Resource Mobilization in Gülen-Inspired Hizmet

Resource Mobilization in Gülen-Inspired Hizmet

A New Type of Social Movement

Sanaa El-Banna

BLUE DOME

16 15 14 13   1 2 3 4

Published by Blue Dome Press
535 Fifth Avenue, Ste. 601
New York, NY 10017-8019

www.bluedomepress.com

Library of Congress Cataloging-in-Publication Data Available

ISBN: 978-1-935295-44-0

Printed by
Çağlayan A.Ş., Izmir - Turkey

Contents

worldwide network of community service organizations, businesses, and educational, publishing and media institutions functioning in more than one hundred countries. In the process of its evolution, the movement has transformed itself from a religious community into a network of professional organizations with an overt universal and humane orientation. Moreover, the movement's Turkish and Islamic background is a cornerstone in strengthening its current humanistic orientation, even though its Turkish dimension is gradually losing its prominence as a result of operating in cosmopolitan environments.

It is not possible to give a very accurate estimate of the size of the movement, but it has been estimated that up to 10 million people in over 100 countries are associated with the movement and its service projects. Because of the voluntary nature of the work performed by movement participants[2] and the autonomy of the institutions they establish, the number of service projects is equally difficult to ascertain. However, best estimates in 2010 suggested that Gülen-inspired institutions comprised over 1,000 schools on five continents; six high quality private hospitals; one private university; several hundred student dormitories and university preparation courses; an international relief organization; and, in every country where the movement is active, many local groups carrying out interfaith and intercultural dialogue.[3] Based on anecdotal evidence I know that these numbers are already out of date and that, for example, by the date of publication of this study several more universities had been founded in Turkey by people inspired by Fethullah Gülen.

In 2008 the movement captured media headlines when Fethullah Gülen won by a landslide *Prospect/Foreign Policy* magazine's online poll the world's most influential public intellectual. *Foreign Policy*'s editor admitted he felt it was a surprise result.[4] This was in spite of the fact that earlier in that same year articles about the movement had already been published in *Oxford Analytica*, the *New York Times*, the *Interna-*

volunteers who contribute with time, skill, money, material support, and knowledge, at multiple levels and at intersecting dimensions of the movement's activism.
...ugh, *The Gülen Movement*, 3.
...://www.prospectmagazine.co.uk/2008/07/howglentriumphed/.

Acknowledgments

This study would not have been possible without the support, guidance and help of several individuals. First and foremost, I am deeply grateful to various Hizmet Movement participants in London who contributed their valuable information and insights during the preparation and completion of this work.

My thanks also extend to my supervisor Dr. Lehmann, in the sociology department of the University of Cambridge, whose inspiration and guidance enabled me to hurdle various obstacles in the completion of this research.

I also thankfully acknowledge the efforts of Dr. İsmail Cebci. His suggestions and comments have prompted and nurtured my intellectual maturity and contributed to the refinement of several drafts of this work.

Words fail me to express my appreciation of my parents, especially my mother, whose prayers turned my worries into hopeful dreams. I am also deeply grateful to all my friends and acquaintances whose support and persistent confidence in me has taken an enormous load off my shoulders.

CHAPTER 1

Muslims in Modernity

This book grew out of my deep interest in [M]
movements, their interaction with modern soci[ety]
response and contributions to global transform[...]
is to explore a part of the work of a peaceful, faith-ins[pir]
tional social movement known as the Hizmet Movemen[t (referred]
to in academia as the Gülen Movement),[1] which rep[resents a]
trend of philanthropic social activism around the wo[rld, grow]
ingly now in the Muslim world.

This particular movement is inspired by a Turkis[h scholar,]
Fethullah Gülen, and became active in Turkey and sub[sequently]
the world from the 1970s onward. My own interest[...]
was piqued between 2007 and 2010, a period in [which]
organizations started to publicize themselves actively[...]
joint projects between El-Nil Center of Language a[nd...]
on one side and the Center for Civilizational Stu[dies...]
Among Cultures in Cairo University on the other. [...]
participated in a major conference titled "The Futu[re of the]
Muslim World: Experiences in Comparison wit[...Move]
ment," the contents of which further stimulated m[...]

Since its inception in Turkey in the 1970s as [...]
hostels and boarding halls, the Hizmet Movemen[t...]

---

[1] The word *hizmet* is a Turkish word of Arabic deriva[tion...]
Movement participants generally expressed their sel[f...]
Movement" or simply "Hizmet" rather than "Gülen [...]
Movement" or "Hizmet" throughout this book becau[...]
impose a loaded term/label on participants' activism wi[...]

Acknowledgments

This study would not have been possible without the support, guidance and help of several individuals. First and foremost, I am deeply grateful to various Hizmet Movement participants in London who contributed their valuable information and insights during the preparation and completion of this work.

My thanks also extend to my supervisor Dr. Lehmann, in the sociology department of the University of Cambridge, whose inspiration and guidance enabled me to hurdle various obstacles in the completion of this research.

I also thankfully acknowledge the efforts of Dr. İsmail Cebci. His suggestions and comments have prompted and nurtured my intellectual maturity and contributed to the refinement of several drafts of this work.

Words fail me to express my appreciation of my parents, especially my mother, whose prayers turned my worries into hopeful dreams. I am also deeply grateful to all my friends and acquaintances whose support and persistent confidence in me has taken an enormous load off my shoulders.

CHAPTER 1

Muslims in Modernity

This book grew out of my deep interest in Muslim social movements, their interaction with modern society, and their response and contributions to global transformation. Its aim is to explore a part of the work of a peaceful, faith-inspired, transnational social movement known as the Hizmet Movement (also referred to in academia as the Gülen Movement),[1] which represents a rising trend of philanthropic social activism around the world and increasingly now in the Muslim world.

This particular movement is inspired by a Turkish Islamic scholar, Fethullah Gülen, and became active in Turkey and subsequently around the world from the 1970s onward. My own interest in the movement was piqued between 2007 and 2010, a period in which some of its organizations started to publicize themselves actively in Egypt through joint projects between El-Nil Center of Language and *Hira'* Magazine on one side and the Center for Civilizational Studies and Dialogue Among Cultures in Cairo University on the other. In October 2009 I participated in a major conference titled "The Future of Reform in the Muslim World: Experiences in Comparison with the Gülen Movement," the contents of which further stimulated my interest.

Since its inception in Turkey in the 1970s as a network of student hostels and boarding halls, the Hizmet Movement has developed into a

---

[1] The word *hizmet* is a Turkish word of Arabic derivation which means "service." Movement participants generally expressed their self-identification as "Hizmet Movement" or simply "Hizmet" rather than "Gülen Movement." I use "Hizmet Movement" or "Hizmet" throughout this book because I found it unacceptable to impose a loaded term/label on participants' activism with which they might disagree.

worldwide network of community service organizations, businesses, and educational, publishing and media institutions functioning in more than one hundred countries. In the process of its evolution, the movement has transformed itself from a religious community into a network of professional organizations with an overt universal and humane orientation. Moreover, the movement's Turkish and Islamic background is a cornerstone in strengthening its current humanistic orientation, even though its Turkish dimension is gradually losing its prominence as a result of operating in cosmopolitan environments.

It is not possible to give a very accurate estimate of the size of the movement, but it has been estimated that up to 10 million people in over 100 countries are associated with the movement and its service projects. Because of the voluntary nature of the work performed by movement participants[2] and the autonomy of the institutions they establish, the number of service projects is equally difficult to ascertain. However, best estimates in 2010 suggested that Gülen-inspired institutions comprised over 1,000 schools on five continents; six high quality private hospitals; one private university; several hundred student dormitories and university preparation courses; an international relief organization; and, in every country where the movement is active, many local groups carrying out interfaith and intercultural dialogue.[3] Based on anecdotal evidence I know that these numbers are already out of date and that, for example, by the date of publication of this study several more universities had been founded in Turkey by people inspired by Fethullah Gülen.

In 2008 the movement captured media headlines when Fethullah Gülen won by a landslide *Prospect/Foreign Policy* magazine's online poll for the world's most influential public intellectual. *Foreign Policy*'s editor admitted he felt it was a surprise result.[4] This was in spite of the fact that earlier in that same year articles about the movement had already been published in *Oxford Analytica*, the *New York Times*, the *Interna-*

---

[2] Volunteers who contribute with time, skill, money, material support, and knowledge, on multiple levels and at intersecting dimensions of the movement's activism.

[3] Ebaugh, *The Gülen Movement*, 3.

[4] http://www.prospectmagazine.co.uk/2008/07/howglentriumphed/.

tional Herald Tribune, *Forbes* magazine, and the *Economist*. The movement had also been examined in a report discussed at the World Economic Forum Annual Meeting in Davos, Switzerland in 2008.[5]

Foreign Policy subsequently published an interview with Gülen[6] in which he categorically renounced the use of violence as a means for political or religious ends, and he became the focus of overwhelming media interest that set his example in contrast to other Islamic intellectuals who had justified, denied, or even celebrated the attack on the US trade centers. A series of dialogue initiatives by the Hizmet Movement then further illustrated its departure from the spectrum of more typical Islamic movements and further opened the movement to participants from different religions, cultures and creeds.

It is obvious then that as part of an influential social movement, Hizmet organizations deserve both wider and closer understanding for the breadth of their goals, the pervasiveness of their projects across decades, their "social movement" qualities and their "glocalizing" orientation. With its primary focus on modern education, quality media outlets, globally-oriented business associations and charitable, interfaith and inter-cultural dialogue activities, the Hizmet Movement profoundly departs from the typical focus of Islamic movements on building an Islamic state, restoring the rule of *shari'a* and reviving the "golden age." They signify a faith-inspired social movement that departs in philosophy and mechanisms from Islamic movements as they are normally viewed. Nevertheless, while compatible with modern philosophy, structures and institutions, the movement's values are deeply rooted in Islamic tradition.

It recognizes the modern nation state[7] as a basis for organizing society, while presenting a curious blend of secularism, modernity, and Islamic values and traditions with an emphasis on the "betterment of human life."

---

5   Ebaugh, *The Gülen Movement*, 3.
6   Tomlin, Meet Fethullah Gülen, the World's Top Public Intellectual.
7   Gülen accepts the existence of the modern nation state but refuses any definition which entails racial, ethnic, cultural, and religious homogeneity "based on some (often imaginary) society in the past." Çetin, *The Gülen Movement*, 143–4.

Classifying the Hizmet Movement

The research reported in this book therefore revolved around a central question: how can the Hizmet Movement be classified in relation to the spectrum of Islamic movements? The study takes the form of an organizational ethnography that explains the movement's know-how in order to define its position *vis-à-vis* Islamic movements in general.

My research drew upon several intertwined lines of enquiry that support the study of Hizmet organizations. These lines include research on Islamic social movements in Turkey and elsewhere; the literature on social movement organizations (SMOs) in general; the literature on the Gülen-inspired Hizmet Movement in particular; and studies of both the Turkish and broader Muslim communities in Britain.

The literature on Islamic social movements in Turkey is specific in that it makes various attempts to examine and explain the impact of a number of socio-historical experiences.[8] A number of emphases have emerged in the literature regarding experiences as diverse and inter-related as: Ottoman modernization, secularism, and nation-state building during the Republican era; political democratization following the implementation of the multi-party system; the bitter experience with military coups in 1960, 1970, 1981, and 1998; the socio-economic liberalization in the 1980s; the rise of political Islam; and recently the study of Turkey's leading Muslim conservative party (or conservative party led by pious Muslim politicians), the AKP.

The disparate streams of research on the Turkish-speaking community in the United Kingdom so far can be seen as falling under a number of themes that are relevant in this study as they were raised by informants. Categories include the history of immigration, identity and culture, associational life, spatial dispersion, inter-ethnic, political and ideological cleavages, and socio-economic problems, which include issues of ethnic economy, women's empowerment, second generation youth, education, crime rates, integration and language concerns.

My work also gained from the large body of research devoted to the study of Islamic movements and Muslim communities in Britain.

---

[8] Şerif Mardin (2005) terms this "Turkish exceptionalism."

Here, it is useful to stress the important caveat that "Islamic identity" is a problematic term in the sense that there is not a culture, and consequently identity, of Islam *per se*. Rather, Islam shapes and gives rise to different cultures.[9] However, Muslim communities in Britain have been subject to academic inquiry over the past decades for two main reasons: firstly, the different socio-economic profile of specific ethnic communities which are overwhelmingly Muslim; secondly, the historical view of Islam in Europe as suspect, which has contributed to the legacy of anti-Muslim sentiment.[10] Muslim communities were further recognized, at local, national, and international levels, following the 9/11 attacks; as a result of media stereotyping, the BNP (British National Party), and the rise of "Islamophobia" in western countries,[11] antagonism and distrust were inflamed between Muslim and other communities including the White majority. The resultant dividing line between "good" and "bad" Muslims further intensified the tension, especially within the Turkish community, over the extent to which religious identity should be preserved, and over the best formula for integration with the broader society.[12]

Finally, contemporary scholarship on the Hizmet Movement, offers obvious assistance on both substantive and methodological levels. A growing number of researchers has contributed to the study of the Hizmet Movement through international conferences, symposia and academic seminars. These cover various aspects of the movement: its philosophy, activities, methods, and strategies, and have tended to depict the movement as a rising trend of modern Islam. While acknowledging their essential subjectivity, these contributions can be broadly classified, in terms of the movement's involvement in their production, into two groups: research by Hizmet-affiliated intellectuals and research carried out in cooperation with the Hizmet Movement.[13]

---

[9] Hellyer 2005:27, cited in Hussain, *Muslims on the Map*, xvi.

[10] Ibid.

[11] Ibid.

[12] Ibid.

[13] Examples of these works include Çetin 2010; Ergene 2005, 2008, 2009; Yavuz and Esposito 2003; Kalyoncu 2006, Kalyoncu 2008; Ebaugh 2009; Hunt 2007; Albayrak

Conference proceedings have covered Gülen's visions on liberalism, secularism, modernity, terrorism, clash of civilizations, jihad and inter-faith dialogue. Researchers have analyzed Gülen's writings using almost every possible academic tradition: political science, philosophy, sociology, theology, economics, education, and linguistic and development studies. Comparisons have been drawn between Gülen and Mevlana Rumi, Tariq Ramadan, Rabbi Abraham Cook, and Abdul-Karim Suroush. Many papers have examined Hizmet networks[14] in different parts of the world. Some contributions have looked at what the Hizmet Movement can "offer." Others have written on such topics as the role of the Hizmet Movement in integrating Turkish minorities and in combating terrorism.[15]

While these studies offer great insight into the research subject in both substantive and methodological respects, an obvious weakness is the dearth of empirical study on the actual activism of the Hizmet Movement. Exceptions to this observation are the works of Çetin and Ebaugh in which interviews, surveys, and observation were deployed to understand the know-how of the movement, although neither focuses directly on its main strength: the organizational aspect.[16] These works provided the groundwork for my study and were especially useful for the study of the Hizmet Movement as a social construct of multiple, overlapping, and variant layers of affiliation with respect to its socio-historical background in Turkey, in its particular environment in London, and in the wider context of Muslim affairs in Britain.

To this literature my study offers a case of a Muslim social movement influenced by its Turkish background in its philosophy and prac-

---

2011; Cantori et al. 2007; Carroll 2007; Celik 2011; Gülen 1995; Hunt and Aslandogan 2007; Khan 2011; Özipek 2010; Saritoprak (Ed.) 2005; Ünal 2000; Sevindi and Abu-Rabi' 2008. The movement has critics and doubters too, e.g., Bishkek and Istanbul 2008; Strauss 2011; Stourton 2011.

14 Informal, multi-layered and intersecting groups "within" the movement that enhance communication and resource mobility.

15 See, for instance, Tedik, Gülen Movement as an Integration Mechanism for Europe's Turkish and Muslim Community, and Tedik, Motivating Minority Integration in the Western Context; also Hussain, Combating Terrorism in Britain.

16 Çetin, *The Gülen Movement*; Ebaugh, *The Gülen Movement*.

tice, by Islamic values and traditions, and by modern philosophy, as well as social and economic structures. Thus, the Hizmet Movement disturbs many established classifications of Islamic Social Movements, by focusing on transnational, humanely articulated, faith-inspired community service, with strong institutional presence and highly organized, diffused business, academic and media networks functioning within local, national and transnational spaces.

Theoretical framework

The study of Social Movement Organizations[17] and organizational commitment theory[18] dates back to the 1970s. Organizational commitment theory places its main focus on how cohesion and solidarity are maintained among the supporting groups of SMOs, assuming that a sense of commitment to an SMO only appears when individuals see the fulfillment of organizational goals as part of their self-fulfillment. A loyal, involved, and committed member sees the movement as an extension of his/her self and sees him/herself also as an extension of the movement. Resource Mobilization Theory places the focus on the rational and strategic aspects of collective action, while other approaches focus on a variety of other aspects: the Political Opportunity and New Social Movement approaches highlight the social movement's environment; the Collective Behavior approach studies the social movement's identity and meaning.

Reflecting multiple concerns rather than a homogenous school of social movements, these approaches often borrow concepts and insights from other fields of study.[19] In line with this tradition, this study focuses on two Social Movement Organizations within the Hizmet Movement that fall within the scope of both the literature on social move-

---

[17] Zald and Ash, *Social Movement Organizations*; McCarthy and Zald, *Resource Mobilization and Social Movements*; McAdam et al. Social Movements; Edwards and McCarthy, Resources and Social Movement Organization.

[18] Kanter, *Commitment and Community*.

[19] Porta and Diani, *Social Movements*, 3.

ments and organizational theory—an overlap where there are three axes of conversion: environmental, cognitive and relational mechanisms.[20]

While the organizational/institutional aspect of Muslim activism is influential, especially in diaspora contexts, the Resource Mobilization literature also proves especially useful for studying Hizmet Movement organizations for a number of reasons: it emphasizes the formal aspects of SMOs; it accommodates their informal mobilization dynamics through social networking; it also recognizes the unique ideational aspect of Muslim activism.[21]

The different methodologies for the study of Islamic Social Movements can be divided into three main approaches: essentialism, contextualism, and constructivism.[22] While essentialism collapses or flattens important distinctions among a group or other unit of analysis, contextualism seeks to relativize phenomena according to the specificity of their context in any given situation. Constructivism, on the other hand, emphasizes "the pluralistic and plastic character of reality; pluralistic in the sense that reality is expressible in a variety of symbol and language systems, and plastic in the sense that reality is stretched to fit purposeful acts of intentional human agents."[23] It is the latter approach, constructivism, that this study employs, in the belief that it offers an effective means of examining the ways in which the Hizmet philosophy is expressed by the Hizmet organizations in London.

The organizational and individual processes of mobilization of the Hizmet Movement are examined as a means of understanding the micro-mobilization mechanisms of Hizmet organizations hosted within the macro-structural determinants of the movement's Turkish context and its current London environment.[24] My analysis also refers to

---

20 Campbell, Where do We Stand?, 44–68.
21 Wiktorowicz, *Islamic Activism and Social Movements Theory*, 208.
22 Yavuz and Esposito, *Turkish Islam and the Secular State*, 16–23.
23 Schwandt, Constructivist, Interpretivist Approaches to Human Inquiry, 128.
24 McCarthy and Zald, The Enduring Vitality of the Resource Mobilization Theory of Social Movements, 534.

a recent typology of resources that categorizes them as moral, cultural, socio-organizational, human and material.[25]

Methodology

The dearth of descriptive material on the actual work of Hizmet organizations invited the study of the subject through qualitative and ethnographic research methods. Ethnography was apt for my research when defined as "a study of people in naturally occurring settings of fields by means of methods which capture their social meaning and ordinary activities, involving the researcher participating directly in the setting, if not also the activities, in order to collect data in a systematic manner but without meaning being imposed on them externally."[26] The qualitative approach is intended to provide an integrated framework for understanding the meaning, context, processes, activities, and events in a way that seeks to make sense of human experiences.[27]

In fact, long before I started my fieldwork, I had already established rapport with movement participants in London (May 2003) through discrete, short visits in which I participated in social and academic events. In these visits, my religious and cultural background, as manifest through my dress code, acquaintance with the Turkish language, as well as religious and Turkish customs, and my position as a female graduate student researching a movement that places ultimate priority on education—including that of young females—greatly raised my "cultural competence,"[28] and facilitated my communication and access to data sources, facilities and accommodation. The ethnographic fieldwork itself took place in March and April, 2011. While carrying it out, I was accommodated consecutively in three places in North London that were managed by or belonged to move-

---

[25] Edwards and McCarthy, informed by Bourdieu's conception of "capital" (Bourdieu 1992, 119 in Edwards and McCarthy, Resources and Social Movement Mobilization, 125).

[26] Brewer, *Ethnography*, 10.

[27] Maxwell, *Qualitative Research Design*, 17–9.

[28] Bourdieu, *Distinction*, 2.

ment participants: a rented hostel of university students, a rented hostel of mosque teachers, and for a short while in a family house.

An important challenge I found was locating Hizmet organizations, since the movement, as far as can be observed, is not subject to definition along ethnic, class, or religious lines. Moreover, the movement adopts flexible and fluid criteria of participation, by which variant degrees of commitment and identification are manifest. Hence, I opted to study the Dialogue Society and the Mevlana Rumi Mosque based on their explicit identification with the philosophy of Gülen, previous research on Turkish associations in London, and primary contacts in Turkey. Therefore, both organizations represent *possible* cases of institutionalized Hizmet activism within an indefinite number of forms that may occur in Britain, Turkey or in other countries; some important examples, such as the *Zaman* newspaper, *The Fountain* magazine and BizNet business associations, were unapproachable due to limitations on time and financial resources.

To gain entry to the two organizations, I chose my primary contacts on the basis of their expected level of experience, engagement in Hizmet activities, and their trustworthiness, that is, their ability to access various events at various levels of the organization in which they took part. In order to ensure the reliability of information, I selected participants according to criteria of age, knowledge and managerial position; that is, to ensure that information was gathered from a number of different vantage points inside the movement, students, housewives, businessmen, managers, teachers, youth and older participants were included in the interviews.

Whether in Turkey or in the United Kingdom, these contacts were asked to give informed personal consent for the fieldwork. I chose to study the Dialogue Society and the Mevlana Rumi Mosque, from among the various independent organizations inspired by the movement, on account of their approachability and prior informed consent to provide information for this research.

As I spent more time in the field, the researcher–respondent divide began to fade away, and I conversed with some informants over long periods of time. Through these conversations, I became aware of crucial aspects of Hizmet through various life biographies involved in its daily life narratives; most importantly, this allowed me to encounter examples of service recipients and financiers who enabled me to develop a more substantial and comprehensive view of different aspects of the two organizations' activism. It was a challenge, however, to maintain the feeling of strangeness or distinctness as I became deeply immersed in the social world of Hizmet. To avoid the dangers of over-rapport,[29] I distanced myself by writing and refining my fieldwork notes where I was unlikely to meet any Hizmet participant that I knew. In addition, I regularly discussed my views with peer scholars who had previously worked on the same movement. By these means I aimed at maintaining a "marginal native"-ness,[30] which allowed me to shift between insider and outsider positions during the fieldwork.

While some informants divulged spontaneous insights and information on Hizmet activities, other Hizmet participants were at first concerned with knowing my research purposes before having any conversations with me. Also, informants in general did not identify themselves directly as part of the Hizmet Movement. My ability to blend in during the fieldwork was greatly deepened by my earlier experiences with the movement in Egypt and Istanbul, Turkey. In addition, knowledge of Turkish cultural codes allowed me to fit in unobtrusively at the social gatherings and daily-life activities: cooking, cleaning, praying, and shopping. This allowed me to develop an authentic and clear understanding of participants' volunteerism as both a social setting and an individual experience. Moreover, it explained and filled the gaps in my interview notes and gave an entrée to individual insights on the work of both organizations as perceived by participants—leaders, workers, and volunteers.

Although most of the study informants welcomed and freely responded to my enquiries, in a few instances, the interviewing/conversation process was daunting as it involved discussing the informant's financial contribution to Hizmet; this was a sensitive issue as talking

---

[29] Miller 1952, 98 in Hammersley and Atkinson, *Ethnography*, 110.
[30] Freilich 1970 in Hammersley and Atkinson, *Ethnography*, 112.

of one's own contribution is seen as threatening the giver's *ihlas* (sincerity or purity of intention), an Islamic notion that is strongly emphasized by Gülen and movement participants. Although informed consent was assured by both organizations' trustees, in some instances, once ordinary participants had realized that I was researching Hizmet Movement organizations, a type of categorizing question preceded, and presumably conditioned the course of, any further conversations; these questions were as direct and sensitive as *"Why are you interested in us?"* or *"What are your claims about the Hizmet Movement?"* Such suspicion can be explained by the politically charged atmosphere around the Hizmet Movement in Turkey, especially in the sensitive period[31] of my fieldwork, as many accusations were being leveled against the movement in Turkish electoral campaigns at that time.[32] In response to these fears, I repeatedly communicated my objective stance toward the movement and the clear need for others to understand how it works in order to eliminate misunderstanding. Finally, while some male informants were extremely cautious and guarded about revealing information, probably out of a compelling sense of responsibility, female informants in general expressed feelings of comfort and trust, probably since they felt that a woman "like themselves" was articulating "their" positions within the organizations. As I spent most of my time with female Hizmet participants—students and teachers—long sociable conversations were facilitated by some informants' need for recognition as a main source of information for my study.[33]

As will be described more fully in later chapters, Hizmet organizations are based on participatory decision making, functional and

---

[31] Ball 1980 in Hammersley and Atkinson, *Ethnography*, 67.

[32] See for instance the attacks by Bahçeli, leader of MHP (The Nationalist Movement Party) on 05/04/2011: http://www.haberturk.com/gundem/haber/617488-bahceli-fethullah-Gülene-cagrisini-yineledi and on 21/05/2011: http://www.cnnturk.com/2011/turkiye/03/31/bahceli.Gülen.cemaati.zan.altinda.kaldi/611764.0/index.html. A thorough summary of the politically motivated prosecutions of Gülen can be found in Harrington 2011.

[33] Bulmer describes this as a case in which perceived 'subjective rewards' underlie an informant's pursuit for equality with the researcher and recognition through providing more information. See Bulmer, *Sociological Research Methods*, 219.

rotating leadership, and flexible structures. While such qualities ensure effective and efficient use of resources, information about the organizations, and most importantly the local knowledge of their functioning, was fairly diffused in multiple narratives that are sometimes inaccurately expressed. To mitigate the drawbacks of this situation, I checked my fieldwork notes by sending summary reports to validate the accuracy of their content and to obtain my informants' consent to using the information in that form. Since the process of interpretation inevitably involved the subjective background of the researcher and the dispositions of earlier research on the movement, data verification, especially in the collection phase, necessitated a "triangulation method."[34] I therefore accounted for multiple sources of evidence through interviewing and observation, and by cross-evaluating interviews, documents, observations, and secondary resources. I regularly consulted informants on the interpretation of their data in the later stages of my research. In addition, I solicited peer as well as academic reviews to ensure greater coherence of the observations and conclusions I reached.

Participant observation was especially important to my study for two reasons. Firstly, interviews at some points generated self-justificatory records about the movement. Secondly, the existence of contradictory opinions about the Hizmet Movement's philosophy, methods and aims necessitated a closer examination of their actual work. Therefore, I examined individual life biographies in order to "reveal the common sense taken for granted as a nature of that everyday world,"[35] that is, through immersion in the life of those who are identified with the phenomenon.[36] In this way, the study deals with Hizmet as a social construct made meaningful within the situations where it is manifest, rather than a stipulated cultural and social system.

---

34 Denzin, *Sociological Methods*, 3.
35 Brewer, *Ethnography*, 58.
36 See Spradley, *Participant Observation* on techniques and skills for ethnography.

Sources of data

The study is based on analysis of two types of primary resources: (1) the writings and recordings of Gülen in Turkish and English, and (2) data culled from ethnographic research in two of the movement organizations in London. Tools of data collection were of two main types: in-depth interviews with informants from the Dialogue Society and the Mevlana Rumi Mosque, and participant observation in Hizmet-managed student dorms, seminars, and local circles and activities of the two organizations in general. Documents, especially regarding the in-house codes of behavior, were used from both organizations.

The study applied a double-tiered interviewing technique with the aim of capturing "true and accurate reflections"[37] on the Hizmet Movement organizations' know-how. While in-depth semi-structured interviews were undertaken with three high-ranking informants with executive positions in the organizations, individuals whose social resources (age, occupation and gender) reflected different weights within the social distribution of the movement's (local) knowledge[38] were identified through the fieldwork period. Various types of Hizmet participant—housewives, students, teachers, academics and business-men—contributed to the study through spontaneous and solicited "conversations with purpose."[39] Though statistically unrepresentative of their spectrum, this group provided a rounded view of the social world of Hizmet through the diverse roles they undertake.

The questionnaire I used was thematically designed around five types of resources: moral, human, socio-organizational, financial and material[40]; also, it was customized to suit each informant's background and functional niche. Most of the interviews, as well as the fieldwork notes, were in Turkish; the use of common language vernaculars raised confidence and trust in the communication process. The study comprised information gathered from sixteen informants in total. In-depth

---

[37] Winlow and Hall 2006, 14 in Van Der Neut, *Change and Continuity on the South Coast*, 14.

[38] Hammersley and Atkinson, *Ethnography*, 137.

[39] Burgess 1984, 102 in Brewer, *Ethnography*, 67.

[40] Edwards and McCarthy, Resources and Social Movement Mobilization, 116–52.

interviews allowed informants to be interviewed in sufficient detail for the results to be taken as reliable, correct, complete, and representative of the organization's goals and mechanisms. The interview process also provided a chance to understand the self-image of Hizmet organizations. Meanwhile, the semi-structured interviewing technique offered a greater degree of latitude to the researcher: dialogic interaction, through discussions and further clarification, was flexibly probed beyond the stipulated themes of my questionnaire. In many instances I "restructured (the) interviews"[41] by changing the order, language, and priority of questions according to the informant's background, interests, and experiences. Since this technique assigned different weights to each theme, the study findings reflected the interests and negotiated priorities of both the researcher and the informants.

In short, I have taken a "micro-ethnographic" approach[42] to studying Hizmet activism as it appears in everyday circumstances, comprising both in-depth interviews and participant observation. The use of flexible resource categories guided the research into various micro mobilization mechanisms as understood and explained within macro socio-historical determinants. In this way, I attempt to apply a "thick description"[43] to the Hizmet Movement by locating the socio-historical contours of its Turkish background, its core philosophical and structural concepts, and its organizational manifestation in its London environment.

Outline of the book

In the next chapter, in order to explain the formative influences on the Hizmet Movement I lay out the main aspects of the movement's socio-historical and political background in Turkey before and during the period in which it emerged. I also present a brief biography of Fethullah Gülen, the scholar who inspires the movement, to shed light on the formal and informal influences on the development of his

---

[41] Pahl 1995, 197–210 in May, *Social Research*, 125.
[42] Bryman, *Social Research Methods*, 403.
[43] Geertz, *The Interpretation of Cultures*, 27.

thought. In chapter 3 I describe the needs and demands of the local constituencies in London, I show how Hizmet organizations are related to those needs and demands, and I compare this relationship to Hizmet's own stipulated goals and forms of activity. In chapter 4 I identify the moral, cultural, human, socio-organizational, and material resources currently mobilized by the Hizmet organizations. Finally, in chapter 5 I offer an analysis of how these resources are mobilized toward realizing the social change the Hizmet Movement calls for. I conclude with an attempt to conceptualize the Hizmet Movement's mobilization mechanisms as what I term "strategic adaptivism," and by this elucidate the movement's distinctive position and characteristics in comparison with the generality of Islamic Movements.

CHAPTER 2

Hizmet in Turkey

Resource mobilization theorists describe two levels of mobilization structures at which social movements can develop: the macro and micro levels.[44] This chapter describes the macro-structural conditions that have shaped the collective action of Turkish Muslims during the last century. It makes two main arguments: firstly, that the collective consciousness of Turkish society was momentously transformed by structural determinants such as top-down secularization and modernization, urbanization, the print revolution, industrialization and political and economic liberalization; and this transformation formed the context for the emergence of *cemaat*s, and in particular, the Hizmet Movement;[45] secondly, I argue that a proper understanding of Gülen's thought requires some appreciation of the three main dimensions that contextualize and shape his text: time, space, and the morphology of their inter-linkages.[46] Other factors in this contextualizing and shaping process are the society in which the text is written, which social realities it addresses, and the intellectual background of the author.[47]

To this end, I examine first the transformation of religious organizations in Turkey under the policies of the new Republic from *madrasa*s and *Sufi* orders toward *cemaat*s, with close discussion of the

---

[44] McAdam et al, *Social Movements*.

[45] Gamson, Fireman and Rytina's work, *Encounters with Unjust Authority*, suggests that successful social movements usually proceed from profound transformations of a similar nature.

[46] Freeden, *Ideologies and Political Theory*, 4.

[47] Skinner, *The Foundations of Modern Political Thought*, xiii.

Nurcu *cemaat* under Said Nursi. I then examine the rise of Gülen's ideas within Turkey's multi-party system, with a select biography of his life, which leads into a brief summary of some of the core philosophical and structural concepts of the Hizmet Movement.

The transformation of *cemaats* under the Republic

Following the founding of the new Republic of Turkey, the period 1923–1928 witnessed a series of social engineering policies enacted by the new Republican regime under Mustafa Kemal Atatürk. Dervish houses were closed, and their ceremonies, liturgy, and traditional dress were outlawed. In 1928, the use of the Latin alphabet for the Turkish language was made obligatory for public authorities, as well as in education and media institutions. A new civil code, penal code, and commercial law replaced the traditional laws inspired by Islamic *shari'a*; these new codes were based on the Swiss, Italian and German codes respectively; and the Gregorian calendar permanently replaced the Islamic *Hijri* calendar.[48]

The laicizing policies of Atatürk eliminated visible attributes of religion in both the public and the private sphere. Modern art and architecture replaced traditional or Ottoman art and architecture, such as the traditional *konak* type of houses. Western customs in clothing were legally enforced, especially on men, and the *ezan*, the Muslim call to prayer, was made in Turkish for eighteen years of the early Republican era.[49]

Meanwhile, the Republican regime also developed new forms of governance for a modern Turkish state—increasing bureaucratization, centralized public administration, legal apparatus, forms of education, and modern agencies of coercion (in particular, the army). Atatürk founded institutions which indoctrinated new definitions of national identity and history. A penetration into the private space of individuals and social groups also started with the enactment of a law that obliged the registration of a Turkish family name for every Turkish

---

[48] Çetin, *The Gülen Movement*, 14.
[49] Ibid., 17.

citizen in 1934. Names of Arabic, Persian, Hebrew, or Armenian origins were prohibited.[50]

A sturdy homogenizing national identity was stressed in the 1924 Constitution, highlighting the Turkish identity of what was an increasingly diverse society in terms of immigrant/returner backgrounds, languages, traditions, and ethnicities. The absence of national consciousness (*maarife-i kavmiye*) according to Ağaoglu[51] was a persistent challenge to Atatürk's assertion of Turkishness as the only national identity for the Republic.[52] The aim of Atatürk's ideology, codified in the Fourth Congress of the People's Republican Party in 1935, was to create a classless, nationalistic (i.e., Turkish) and secular society, in which sources of difference, religion and ethnicity, were eliminated. The one-party system from 1920 to 1950 took further steps to bring religion under the full control of the state.[53]

Following the death of Atatürk in 1938, the mounting social and political tensions during the early Republican decades were further intensified by İsmet İnönü's[54] economic and financial policies. Resentful attitudes rose against the single-party authoritarianism, and the Democratic Party, which started Turkey's multi-party system, brought a series of agricultural and financial reforms along with a relative release of state censorship over the media. Religion-friendly public policies under Democratic Party rule, coupled with the spread of print technology, eventually broadened the public sphere, accommodated Islamic publications and facilitated the recurrence of the *cemaat*s in Turkish society.

In many of its attributes, the *cemaat* system—out of which the Nursi and the Gülen *cemaat*s arose—replicated the basic features of

---

[50] Ibid. The 'purification' policy during Ataturk's Republic targeted the 'cleansing' of Persian and Arabic traces from the Turkish language—a process that led to impoverishing the Turkish language of its rich resources and forced Turkish intellectuals to resort to English and French words to fill that linguistic gap (Mardin, Playing Games With Names, 125).

[51] A Turkish intellectual, politician and historian.

[52] Shissler, *Between Two Empires*, 167.

[53] Çetin, *The Gülen Movement*, 18–20.

[54] An army general and the second president of the Turkish Republic in 1938.

the *Ulema* (Islamic scholars) and *Sufi* traditions in Turkey. By definition, the *Ulema* are "mediators between the Holy Scripture's interpretations and the masses' system."[55] They specialized in communicating the "high language" of the Scriptures to popular culture and social practices.[56] Filling the gap left by the *Ulema*'s weakened social and political significance, the *cemaat* system was based on popular and non-differentiated groups of Muslims who gathered around religious scholars, without formal membership, initiation rites, or a specific place for convention.[57] This system made use of the remaining social capital of *Sufi* orders and enabled a purposeful accumulation of religious knowledge for the rural Turkish population, which had limited access to national education.[58] In their effort to counter-balance the repercussions of urban migration on personal and collective identity, especially the rising norms of alienation and anonymity, *cemaat*s replaced *Sufi* lodges with "mosque communities," and *tarikat*s (*Sufi* orders) were replaced by civic organizations.[59]

The first and most prominent *cemaat* that witnessed the Republican transformations was led by Said Nursi (1873–1960). Although he was a pro-parliament republican, his *cemaat* represented an early societal rejection of the Young Turks' un-Islamic reforms. The core of Nursi's ideas is the revival of Islamic faith and the social responsibility of Muslims in the face of the sweeping norms of individualization, atheism and materialism.[60] His magnum opus, *Risale-i-Nur*, is a series of Qur'anic commentaries in which he restates the basics of faith, morality, and ideal social conduct in Muslim communities. During the Democratic Party's tenure in the 1950s, his *Risale-i-Nur* became

---

[55] Gilsenan, *Recognizing Islam*, 30.

[56] Ibid., 51.

[57] The *cemaat*s' activism was greatly eased after the abolition of articles 141, 142 and 163 from the Turkish constitution during the 1980s (see Kilinc, The Patterns of Interaction Between Islam and Liberalism, 132).

[58] Mardin, *Religion and Social Change in Modern Turkey*, 25–8 and Bulaç, The Most Recent Revival in the 'Ulama Tradition, 102.

[59] Ergene, The Future of Islamic Movements in the Arab World.

[60] Mardin, *Bediüzzaman Said Nursi Olayı*, 262.

widely accessible, leading to a coherent *cemaat* of his students and the recognition of his teachings for their wide implications regarding social and political life in Turkey.[61]

Through its dialogical methodology, the *Risale-i Nur* aimed at three interrelated goals: "(1) to raise Muslims' religious consciousness; (2) to refute the dominant intellectual discourses of materialism and positivism; and (3) to recover collective memory by revising the shared grammar of society, Islam."[62]

Nursi was an advocate of a pro-reconciliatory social activism that accommodates modern and traditional values and refutes perceived contradictions among them. This approach has been strongly endorsed by the Gülen-inspired Hizmet Movement around Turkey that draws upon the enormous social and moral capital of Nursi's traditions. In his introduction to *Risale-i Nur*, Gülen highlights Nursi's views on faith, science and human nature, and encourages the establishment of an institution through which the *Risale-i Nur* would become accessible to a wider range of readers.[63]

The later emergence of the "intellectual-*'Ulema*" who have acquired knowledge from both religious and secular sources further supported Nursi's line of thought; this was mainly prefigured in Gülen's background, which facilitated a profound understanding of both religious and modern philosophies.[64]

A select biography of Fethullah Gülen

M. Fethullah Gülen was born in 1941, in a small village near Erzurum, in eastern Turkey, an area known for its conservative culture and *Sufi* traditions,[65] and described by Gülen as a village where poverty, scarcity, and drought was prevalent.[66] He completed his early sec-

61 Vahide, Bediüzzaman Said Nursi and the Risale-i Nur, 33–5.
62 Yavuz and Esposito, *Turkish Islam and the Secular State*, 7
63 In Gülen's introduction to Said Nursi's *Mathnawi al-Nuriya*, xx–xxviii.
64 Bulaç, The Most Recent Revival in the 'Ulama Tradition, 113.
65 Ebaugh, *The Gülen Movement*, 23.
66 Erdoğan, *Fethullah Gülen Hocaefendi 'Küçük Dünyam'* translated in part in Ünal, *Advocate of Dialogue*, 10.

ular education at primary school. However, his further formal schooling was prevented by his father's appointment as an imam in a different province where, because of distance, secondary education was not then accessible to him.[67] He received instead informal education from his parents and the scholars of his town, and was introduced to *Risale-i Nur* through Nursi's students.[68] Gülen remembers that his first teacher was his mother, a Qur'an teacher in the village, who trained him in correct Qur'anic recitation.[69] His father, Ramiz Efendi, was an imam with close connections to the *Nakshibendi tarikat* in Erzurum.[70] He taught Gülen both Persian and Arabic,[71] and gave him entrée to the world of Islamic thinkers such as al-Hasan al-Basri, Harith al-Muhasibi, al-Ghazali, Jelaluddin Rumi, Ahmed Faruk Sirhindi, Shah Wali Allah al-Dihlawi.[72] Gülen later came under the tutelage of (Alvarli) Muhammad Lütfi Efendi, a member in the *Kadiri Sufi* order[73] who, according to Gülen, greatly influenced his intellectual development.[74]

In fact, the *Nakshibendi* background of his tutors is especially important in the sense that it represents an influential "part of Turkish history, culture, economics, politics, and individual identity for several centuries (…) and a repository of virtually all cultural and religious traditions that have existed in Turkey."[75] While this background explains the increasingly spiritual curve of his thought, manifest in his four-volume masterpiece, *Key Concepts in the Practice of Sufism: the Emerald Hills of the Heart*, Gülen never took part in a *Sufi* order (or *tarikat*) and strongly resists characterizing Hizmet as a *tarikat* or *Sufi* order centered around a *shaykh*. Indeed, he has often criticized the *tarikats* for cultivating individual passivity toward social responsibilities.

---

[67] Ebaugh, *The Gülen Movement*, 23.
[68] Ünal, ibid., 15.
[69] Erdoğan, *Fethullah Gülen Hocaefendi 'Küçük Dünyam'* translated in part in Ünal, *Advocate of Dialogue*, 13.
[70] Saritoprak and Griffith, Fethullah Gülen and the "People of the Book", 330.
[71] Ünal, *Advocate of Dialogue*, 11.
[72] Saritoprak and Griffith, Fethullah Gülen and the "People of the Book", 331.
[73] Ibid., 330.
[74] In Ünal, *Advocate of Dialogue*, 10.
[75] Yavuz, *Islamic Political Identity in Turkey*, 134.

Gülen, rather, envisages Sufism as the spirit of Islam, "a path followed by individuals for the pursuit of deeper understanding of the Qur'anic message."[76] Guided by the practice of the Prophet's companions, it is the way that leads individuals to better engagement in their society through constituting role models of absolute self-sacrifice.

Gülen pursued his secular education in positive sciences, literature, history and philosophy through informal self-education. During his military service, his commander recommended a number of major thinkers for his reading.[77] Among the writers whose work he encountered this way were Hugo, de Balzac, Kant, Shakespeare and Einstein, and French existentialist philosophers such as Sartre and Camus, as well as Marcuse's critique of modernity and Shakespeare's plays.[78] With this background, he would later develop his thoughts on reconciling modernity and spirituality through Islamic values.

Gülen's rural and Anatolian background also draws attention to "Anatolian Muslimness" as a major input in his formation. Anatolian Muslimness,[79] described in terms of cultural and liturgical practices, is characterized by: (1) mediation, mainly between the meaning of the Arabic Scripture and Turkish-speaking Muslims, (2) *mürşid*/guide centrality,[80] and (3) rootedness in regional and ascetic ideals as cultivated through the work of classical poets such as Alvarlı, Mehmet Akif, Necip Fazıl, Erol Güngör, Sezai Karakoç and other Turkish poets. This input helps to explain how Gülen has such a strong influence on the general public through his sermons, poetry and writings.

---

[76] Michel, The Gülen Movement.

[77] Çetin, *The Gülen Movement*, 31; and Ünal, *Advocate of Dialogue*, 19.

[78] Ünal, *Advocate of Dialogue*, 16.

[79] The term refers to a type of Muslimness/Muslimhood that accommodates differences and institutionalizes co-existence in social, economic, and political institutions. It holds that the Anatolian region was exposed to many cultures, faiths and communities both before and during its Ottoman history. According to Gülen (2004a) it has been able to preserve much of these cultural and religious traditions by escaping the European colonial complex. It therefore differs from other types of Muslimhood that grew in culturally homogeneous environments and envision a single straight norm of religiosity that reflects their social and historical settings.

[80] In Sufism the seeker (*mürid*) is the student of the guide (*mürşid*) in the *tarikat*.

Ottoman history shows in Gülen's background through his assertion that Ottomans modeled Islamic values through their spirit of dialogue; their multilingual, multi-ethnic and multi-religious society; their respect for women; and the cultural rapprochement between Ottoman society and the West during the nineteenth century.[81] In addition to the Millet system of the Ottoman rule, mutual recognition of the different segments of society was also inculcated by the traditional Sufi Masters that are repeatedly cited in his writings, such as Yunus Emre, Ahmed Yesevi, Haji Bayram-i Veli, and Akşemseddin (the Sufi master of Sultan Mehmet the Conqueror).[82] In some of his articles, Gülen vividly describes the Ottoman civilization as one with qualities of "the mind, heart, and spirit."[83]

While sociologist Elisabeth Özdalga defines three reference points for Gülen's thought—Sunni Islam, Nakshibendi Sufi traditions, and the Nurculuk movement[84]— his biography suggests a wider input space in addition to his experience as an official preacher since the 1960s. In this regard, Skinner underlines a number of factors that help to identify wider input spaces and that better explain the momentous spread of an intellectual's ideas around the world: "what the intellectual was *doing*" in writing his text, what question he is addressing, and how he utilizes the concepts available to him.[85] The following paragraphs provide a more rounded grasp of Gülen's thought through examining these factors.

In 1960, Gülen was granted official status as a preacher of the Turkish Directorate of Religious Affairs.[86] Throughout the 1960s and 1970s, he held posts in Edirne, Kırklareli, and İzmir and the Aegean region. At the same time as providing a fairly broad exposure to the different sub-cultural and urban systems of modern Turkey, this experience also informed his discourse with both general and particular

---

[81] Ebaugh, *The Gülen Movement*, 33.

[82] Saritoprak and Griffith, Fethullah Gülen and the "People of the Book", 332.

[83] Ünal, *Advocate of Dialogue*, 5.

[84] Özdalga, Worldly Asceticism in Islamic Casting, 91.

[85] Skinner, *The Foundations of Modern Political Thought*, xiii.

[86] Erdoğan, *Fethullah Gülen Hocaefendi 'Küçük Dünyam.'*

acquaintances among his audience. Moreover, Gülen preached in coffee shops, village gatherings, workplaces, and organized camps for students in middle and high school.[87] The subjects of his sermons ranged from education, science, Darwinism, economy and social justice to more theological subjects of the Islamic faith, which later crystallized in his main argument: "our three greatest enemies are ignorance, poverty, and internal schism."[88]

With the spread of his ideas on education and charitable support for needy students, Gülen inspired the establishment of a bursary and student hostel system known as "lighthouses" (*ışık evleri*). Support was received from local working and middle-class groups, which set up study circles around the ideas of Gülen. By these means, Hizmet ethics started to spread steadily across the whole Anatolian region, where his supporters, then barely a hundred working class individuals, formed the core of what was later known as the Hizmet Movement.[89]

The movement's first university preparatory courses were established in 1974 in Manisa, where Gülen was posted at that time. Following the success of such initiatives, Gülen was called upon to preach in different parts of Turkey, where local communities were becoming enormously hopeful about the future of their children. Moreover, in 1979, *Sızıntı* started as a monthly journal which, among other topics, expressed Gülen's ideas about the reconciliation of faith with secular education, with the nation state, and with democracy. Gülen provided the editorial section from the beginning, elaborating on the relationship between Islam, Sufism and the meaning of faith in modern life.[90]

In the 1980s Turkey, led by Turgut Özal, also witnessed an unprecedented economic and political liberalization that gave rise to a new class of technocrats, professionals, businessmen, and wealthy entrepreneurs,[91] who combined religious conservatism with qualified

---

[87] Çetin, *The Gülen Movement*, 31.
[88] Gülen, *Toward a Global Civilization of Love and Tolerance*, 198.
[89] Çetin, *The Gülen Movement*, 33–43.
[90] Ibid., 37.
[91] Ibid., 170.

education and profound orientation toward the Hizmet ethos as pro-
moted by Gülen[92]; this class found Gülen's message acceptable due to
his use of strong traditional Islamic arguments from the Qur'an and
Sunnah (*Kurani Makuliyet*). In later decades this sector of society
evolved into the "Anatolian bourgeoisie" that sets up and finances the
Hizmet Movement's schools and charitable organizations.[93] With Özal's
new socio-economic policies, a "market friendly religio-education
movement"[94] started to gain organizational and institutional momentum. Gülen's sermons during the 1980s drew large crowds of supporters, who also videotaped his lectures and broadcast and transcribed
them for the larger population of conservative Turks.[95]

The social and cultural constituency for Gülen's ideas was further
multiplied after the collapse of the former Soviet Union in the early
1990s, and the consequent liberation of many Turkic nations in the
Central Asian and Balkan regions. The concepts of tolerance, human
rights, education, and dialogue, which had hitherto comprised the
themes of Gülen's writings, became ideally suitable for his new listen-
ers in the multi-ethnic Turkic societies.

In 1994, the Journalists and Writers Foundation was established
Since the late 1990s, the Journalists and Writers Foundation has been
contributing to the diffusion of Hizmet strategies of consultation and
consensus-building through the *Abant* Platforms.[96] These annual forums
have engaged a wide network of academicians, journalists and intellectuals from across the political spectrum in discussions about a national and/or international issue. At the end of each meeting the platform
releases a statement which has been reached by consensus.

Also in 1994, Gülen made visits to preach in Turkish mosques and
community centers around the world, especially in the United States

---

[92] Ibid., 43. This class also gave rise to parallel initiatives whose organizational techniques resembled Hizmet's but had different ideational set-ups, such as the Republican
Youth (Milli Gençlik) and Knowledge Disseminating (Ilim Yayma) initiatives that
later crystallized into charitable institutions.

[93] Yilmaz, Beyond Post-Islamism, 914.

[94] Yavuz and Esposito, *Turkish Islam and the Secular State*, 35.

[95] Çetin, *The Gülen Movement*, 46.

[96] Named after Abant, the place where the first platform convened.

and European countries.[97] Gülen-inspired schools, media enterprises, and business associations began to spread in the Balkan and Central Asian regions. Gülen also inspired the establishment of a chain of economic and media outlets, including the Association for Solidarity in Business Life (ISHAD) and the Businessmen's Association for Freedom (HURSIAD) in 1993, and the Turkish Businessmen and Industrialists Confederation (TUSKON), all of which paved the way toward establishing schools and trade initiatives all over the world, and also created mutual interests between the movement and subsequent Turkish regimes.[98]

Gülen's positive views on inter-faith and inter-cultural dialogue had been expressed publicly as far back as 1998 with his visit to Pope John Paul II and continuously since that time. The 9/11 attacks on the United States gave further impetus to Hizmet's dialogue work after the movement and its participants were recognized by Western policy makers as a potential means of promoting understanding and coexistence within Western societies—mainly between Muslim communities and the larger "indigenous" community.[99] Hizmet further extended its model of "*Sufi*-type modern spirituality"[100] to the post-9/11 world and created an immensely active transnational network of dialogue NGOs and educational services in many areas of the world previously untouched by its work.

Structural and operational concepts of Hizmet

Within the Hizmet Movement, Gülen is perceived as a profound scholar (*'alim*). His personal qualities such as "humility, asceticism and dedication to good deeds (*al-'amal al-salih*)" revive the *Suffa* traditions of the early Islamic centuries.[101] Gülen's example of "lead(ing) a single, sim-

---

[97] Ibid.

[98] Ibid.

[99] See for instance speeches by former US president Bill Clinton and others on www. Gülen institute.org/.

[100] Michel, The Gülen Movement.

[101] "The *Suffa* Companions...comprised...single young men who...were provided with shelter and food in the Prophet's Mosque in Medina. Their sole occupation was to

ple (poor), humble and pious life dedicated to God in all aspects"[102] iconizes the Hizmet notions of sacrifice and altruism (*diğergamlık*). These qualities are communicated through Gülen's informal "school," in which he instructs and teaches Islamic sciences—theology (*kalam*), Qur'anic exegesis (*tafsir*), methodology of hadith (*usul al-hadith*) and Islamic jurisprudence (*fiqh*) to Turkish theology graduates.[103]

The rest of this chapter will describe briefly the core concepts of the Hizmet Movement.

Local circles (*sohbet*)

Sohbet is a Turkish word used to refer to a range of cultural processes that include "pleasant conversation or a facial and verbal communication on a certain subject with a group of fellow friends."[104] In the Hizmet Movement a normative dimension of its meaning, one that distinguishes *sohbet*s from ordinary meetings, is that *sohbet*s are developed and nurtured among friends and brothers (or sisters) who seek advancement of their religious and social knowledge through warm communication. Organized around locality and profession, participants in *sohbet*s study passages from various sources. A *sohbet* may start with reading selective parts of the Qur'an, explaining their theme, and studying the relevant parts of Said Nursi's *Risale-i Nur*, a commentary on the Qur'an. Discussions may also refer to prophetic traditions, other exegeses and Gülen's writings.[105]

The aim of a *sohbet* is to gather individuals from similar backgrounds in order to:

1) Strengthen faith (*iman*), develop a better understanding of religion (Islam) and heighten a sense of social responsibility;

---

spend all their time with the Prophet, learning and studying. They became so well versed in Islam that most of them were sent as teachers and/or governors to new provinces." Atay, Reviving the *Suffa* Tradition, 465.

[102] Ibid., 465–7.

[103] Ibid.

[104] Translated from "Görüşüp konuşma, karşılıklı hoşça konuşma." Source:www.risaleinurenstitusu.org.

[105] Kalyoncu, *A Civilian Response to Ethno-Religious Conflict*, 34.

2) Develop common understanding of Hizmet-related principles and values through discussing Gülen's writings;

3) Develop strong inter-personal relations: since a *sohbet* is held in small numbers, individuals have a chance to lead and actively participate with opinions, reflections and experiences;

4) Develop channels for mutual benefit among participants, e.g. businessmen who develop their knowledge of potential partners, customers and suppliers;

5) Emulsify individual opinions and moderate extremist views on religious matters.

Collective decision making and board of trustees (*istişare* and *mütevelli heyeti*)

In the Hizmet Movement collective decision making (*istişare*) is performed on a consensual basis by participants in a network, activity or project. Gülen is known to apply this norm to his own activities and to encourage his students and friends to follow this practice.[106] In addition, every project, business or activity has a *mütevelli heyeti*—essentially a board of trustees that comprises managers and financiers who "consistently carry out the responsibilities that fall on (their) shoulders."[107]

Personal commitment and passion for giving (*himmet* and *verme tutkusu*)

Himmet denotes personal commitment and enthusiasm to carry out a project with best results. Operationally, it refers to the act of contribution, financially or otherwise, to a project and maintenance of such contributions over long periods of time. Every year, the principals of a project gather and openly announce the amount of time, effort, goods or money they are intending to donate. In such meetings, participants are encouraged by seeing each other's enthusiasm to contribute money, time and effort, and individuals strive to contribute as much as they can from whatever resources they have; the "passion for giving" and

---

[106] See, for instance, Gülen, *The Statue of Our Souls*, 37.
[107] Kalyoncu, *A Civilian Response to Ethno-Religious Conflict*, 37.

competition in this are repeatedly reported of participants, especially those with longer experience in the Hizmet Movement.

Donation and migration (*sadaka* and *hicret*)

Through his writings and sermons, Gülen has developed a new definition of *sadaka* and *vakıf* (charity foundation) as financial concepts of Islamic thought. While donations in Islamic law are made for nine social groups, and are normally divided into obligatory donations (*zakat*) and voluntary donations (*sadaka*), both types of giving have been redefined in such a way that makes *zakat* applicable to skills, knowledge, time, and wealth. Also, for various community service activities, eliminating the barriers of understanding and communication as well as prejudice and stereotypes has been presented as a norm of *sadaka* equal in its obligation and reward to traditional forms of *zakat*.

Consequently, the Hizmet Movement draws on a financial and material body of contributions, in which participants not only encourage voluntary charity (*sadaka*) and donation in their normal ranges (*zakat* is due on 2.5% of wealth according to Islamic law), but also urge more substantial and varied tangible donations (time, effort, skill, knowledge, etc.) so as to realize the movement's philosophy.

As it founds educational, business, media, cultural and academic institutions in different societies,[108] the Hizmet Movement also relies on the *hicret* (migration) of its participants to places where volunteerism is necessary, in order to provide services for local communities.[109]

Good conduct (*edep*)

Edep,[110] according to Gülen, enables individuals to enact ascetic or *Sufi* values in their everyday life in what he considers to be the *Sufi* way of

---

[108] Ergene, *Geleneğin Modern Çağa Tanıklığı*, 382.

[109] Since participants opt for and/or are encouraged to travel in pursuit of either their studies, businesses, or for their self-fulfillment as community servants, they inevitably gain wider exposure to different languages, cultures, and faiths, which contributes to the more humanistic approach of the movement's members compared to other social movements. Gülen further lays out this concept in *Umit Burcu*, 173–6.

[110] Turkish word derived from Arabic; commonly transliterated into English as *adab*.

life.[111] Through his writing and practice, Gülen stresses norms of humility (*tevazu*), self-control, self-criticism (*muhasebe*), and piety. The individual ascent through stages of spiritual purification is taught by Gülen through a self-disciplining strategy—less speech, less sleep, and less eating. On its own this would lead a person influenced by Gülen to lead a reclusive life but then Gülen balances this with emphasis on proactive engagement and activism which results in an interesting personality—one that is spiritual and worldly at the same time. Gülen also preaches the necessity of smiling, and of seeing the best in others (*hoşgörü*), as a fundamental means of social communication.[112] Abstention from deliberate direct criticism of any behavior or thought of another, as well as silence, is considered among the pillars of *edep* teachings that are primarily manifest in his own character.[113]

Embodiment of ideals vs. direct preaching (*temsil* vs. *tebliğ*)

Deliberate preaching about what "Islam says" (proselytism) is strongly discouraged by Gülen. In Gülen's view, such proselytism creates a superiority–inferiority complex between those who know and those who do not. Moreover, the psychological resistance which has grown in the global environment due to Islamophobic campaigns is likely to result in mounting hostility toward proselytizers (those who practice *tebliğ*).[114] Instead of verbal "witnessing," a fundamental norm of Hizmet activism is the embodiment or exemplification of Islamic values and ideals in an individual's daily life (*temsil*).

Just ends and means (*maqasid* and *maslaha*)

The blend of intellectual and life experiences in Gülen's background suggests a certain harmony with what Islamic scholars have been developing as the *maqasid* approach since the twelfth century. The term

---

[111] Gülen, *Toward a Global Civilization of Love and Tolerance*, 166.
[112] Gülen, *The Statue of Our Souls*, 72.
[113] Toğuslu, Gülen's Theory of Arab and Ethical Values of Gülen Movement.
[114] Ergene, *Geleneğin Modern Çağa Tanıklığı*, 385.

maqasid refers to purposes, objectives, or principles that lie behind Islamic rulings.[115] Such principles are classified in various ways. One of them is "the preservation of the soul, wealth, mind, offspring and honor" of human beings (Al-Shatebi), and some scholars, such as Al-Qarafi (d.1285), state a fundamental rule regarding the application of these principles: "*Al-maqasid*, the purpose, is not valid unless it leads to the fulfillment of some good, *maslaha*, or the avoidance of some mischief, *mafsada*."[116]

Fulfilling the good, or *maslaha*, is defined by Gülen, in a positive way, as the betterment of humankind through reforming existing systems of modern education, economy and media. In a negative definition, Hizmet is the practice that eliminates ignorance, poverty, and internal schism. It is about the realization of a quality of life, in which Islamic values and traditions are integrated within modern, national and global, political and economic structures. Gülen's approach toward defining and realizing *maslaha* acknowledges the restrictions upon human will in the pursuit of perfection. In this way, the "ought to be" is adapted, in its meaning, aims, methods, and policies, to specific contexts. Apart from its chief goal (that is, glorifying the word of God—*i'layı kelimetullah*—and commitment to religious duties in private life) Hizmet applies a meaning of *maslaha* that is relative, vulnerable, and temporal. At the same time, it takes the traditional approach to *maqasid*, by which the rulings of Islam are examined in relation to their further objectives, in order to realize the betterment of human life. For instance, by these means, schisms between observant Muslims and the outside world are mitigated through intercultural and inter-faith dialogue activities. Similarly, the movement promotes structures that perfectly suit the *maslaha* of the societies where it functions, such as integration into the global economy, and endorsement, internalization and even defense of democracy and rule of national law, and passive secularism that enables active expression of religious feeling in the public sphere.

---

[115] Auda, *Maqasid Al-Shariah*, 2.
[116] In ibid., 2.

Conclusion

In conclusion, to counter the three main problems of his society—ignorance, poverty, and internal schism—Gülen advocated three themes of activism: quality education, ethical entrepreneurship, and inter-faith and intercultural dialogue initiatives. Media outlets—television and radio channels, publishing houses, websites and international conferences—communicated his thought and mobilized wider support for these activities. One result of this dense web of activism was the emergence of the Hizmet Movement in virtually every part in the world his words had reached. A wide variety of philanthropic and business projects have taken place on the basis of Gülen's ideal of community service.

This chapter has focused on the macro-level socio-political and historical determinants in Turkey within which the movement emerged, with the aim of understanding the social actor's original environment, its specific background and the main conceptual and structural components of its discourse. These aspects of the movement are the broader narrative to the movement's micro-mobilizational aspects. They also constitute the sense of collective identity shared among different networks of the Hizmet Movement. From that "collective" identity, in the next chapter, I move on to discussing the "particular" about the Hizmet organizations in London, specifically their resources and which mechanisms underlie their functioning.

CHAPTER 3

Hizmet in London

This chapter examines the micro-mobilizational aspects of Hizmet organizations and the factors that affect their mobilizability, such as participants' prior contact, membership in other organizations, history of previous activism, and biographical availability as affected by such factors as employment, marriage and family responsibilities. First, however, it is necessary to give a brief introduction to the socio-organizational context of the London Turkish community, and the Muslim community in general in order to understand the particular environment of the Hizmet organizations. This chapter will also illustrate some of the needs and demands of the local constituencies in London and the ways in which Hizmet organizations relate to them with respect to their stipulated goals and activity forms.

Hizmet's socio-economic background in London

In this section, I first provide an overview of the evolution of Muslim associations in the United Kingdom, and then address the social composition of the Turkish community. The associational life of the Turkish community in London is generally placed within a context of highly fragmented and politicized Muslim organizations that started earlier and therefore colored the scene for Turkish associations.

Muslim organizations in Britain emerged on local and national levels out of collective and mounting concerns about social, cultural, and political issues. Collective attempts to institutionalize community service and influence state policies emerged after the "myth of return" started to fade away.[117] Target state policies included those relating to educational religious establishments (mosques and *madrasas*) and aspects of morality, laws of personal affairs, and codes of behavior and morality.[118] The first mosque in London was established in 1940. After some time the number of mosques began to rise rapidly as different Muslim communities tended to establish their own mosques and community centers. This added to a rising trend of fragmentation and concentration around specific ethnic, cultural, and religious affiliations. Muslim organizations were firstly occupied with matters of personal morality and collective welfare, such as worship, dress, health, and diet. Soon afterwards, their focus shifted toward *da'wa*[119] and survival of faith; this shift in focus turned mosques from simple religious facilities into centers of social and political activism.[120]

The inclusiveness of mosques became questionable as they began to identify with specific schools of Islam *(madhhabs)* or communities *(jamaats)*; for instance, the Deobandi *Tablighi Jamaat* was associated with the *Tablighi Markaz* at Dewsbury aiming at converting Britain to Islam through the call to Islam *(tabligh* or *da'wa)*.[121] The United Kingdom Islamic Mission, which is known to be close to the *Jamaat-e Islami* and which is also organized around the mission of *da'wa*, has expanded into as many as seventeen British cities and functioned as a mediator between the local authorities and Muslim communities. Its early focus on education culminated in the establishment of the Muslim Educational Trust (MET) in the beginning of the 1970s to deal with government policies that concern Muslim students in public schools.[122] Various Sufi orders and youth organizations also emerged around different groups and approaches to religious expression and practice.[123]

---

[117] Ansari, *The Infidel Within*, 346.

[118] Ibid., 354.

[119] Arabic-derived word meaning broadly "invitation (to the faith)."

[120] Ibid., 344.

[121] Ibid., 348.

[122] Both *Tablighi Jamaat* and *Jamaat-e Islami* serve and are run mainly by people of South Asian/Pakistani origin.

[123] Ansari, *The Infidel Within*, 345–354.

This highly fragmented and hybrid map of Muslim associations is reflected in Turkish associational life too. The Turkish community in London is composed of three broad socio-economic and ethnic groups: Turkish Cypriot, Mainland Turkish, and Kurdish. All three groups are known for their "superdiversity" and multiple, contentious, and overlapping identities, reflected through diverse ethnic, political, cultural, and religious affiliations.[124] This is clearly mirrored in the associational and spatial dispersion of these communities.

A sociological assessment of the settlement pattern of Turkish minorities reveals highly concentrated "parallel societies" living in northeast London (Hackney, Haringey, Enfield and Islington) and south London (Southwark and Lewisham).[125] Haringey and Stoke Newington are generally known for having leftist, Kurdish or Kurdish Alevi minorities, while the Newington Green area is known as a rightist-nationalist neighborhood occupied by supporters of *Ülkücü Hareket* (the Idealist Movement) and the MHP (the Nationalist Action Party).[126]

The Cyprus Turkish Association, founded in 1951, placed minor emphasis on issues of religion and faith, and this perceived gap gave rise to the United Kingdom Turkish Islamic Association in 1979.[127] Following the establishment of the *Aziziye* Mosque in London in 1983, the different sub-groups of the Turkish community began to organize around specific religious and ethnic inclinations and establish multi-purpose organizations in a way that mirrored the pace of Muslim communities' associational evolution in general: inclusiveness, then fragmentation.[128]

Religious-ideological affiliation further divided the Turkish-speaking community; lying at the heart of the Turkish Islamic identity, Turkish mosques such as *Aziziye*, *Sülemaniye* and *Fatih* were established by different religious affiliations, standing independent from and implicitly competing with other ideological standpoints. Mosque polity is large-

---

[124] Tayfun, "Ethnicity Within Ethnicity" Among Turkish Speaking Immigrants in London.

[125] Cilingir, Identity and Integration among Turkish Sunni Muslims in Britain.

[126] Ibid.

[127] Ansari, *The Infidel Within*, 351.

[128] Ibid., 352–3.

ly organized around specific figures, such as Shaykh Nazim of the Turkish Cypriot community, or Mahmut Hoca and Süleyman Hilmi Tunahan of the Turkish mainlanders. In addition to these figures, the Turkish Directorate of Religious Affairs also plays an active role in organizing sermons, religious programs, and providing teachers and imams for different Turkish mosques.[129]

As for the Alevi community, it is generally at odds with Sunni Muslims. Alevis include both Turkish and Kurdish immigrants and are widely described as a heterodox, syncretic, worldly, and relatively liberal sect among Turkish minorities.[130] However, a recent split has demarcated further sub-borders within the community. On one side, the moderate Alevis in London are generally affiliated to the England Alevi Cultural Centre and *Cem Evi*. On the other, the more leftist-socialist Alevis have initiated their own organization (England Alevi Institute) which holds more radical and dissident positions.[131]

Turkish community centers are no different. Reflecting different clientele profiles and membership categories, they are identified with their members' and managers' backgrounds, and these organizations undertake an identical multi-purpose set of activities: welfare, education, language, and socio-religious and cultural events. As a result, sub-cultural boundaries are maintained and even developed into closed enclaves of impoverished socio-economic and geographical categories.

Another theme should be incorporated into this preview. Since the late 1980s, the rise of umbrella Muslim associations, such as the Union of Muslim Organizations in the United Kingdom and Ireland (UMO), the Council of Mosques (COM), the United Kingdom Action Committee on Islamic Affairs (UKACIA), and the Muslim Council of Britain (MCB) have reflected the need for national unity among Muslim associations to represent their demands adequately and influence government policies and legislation.[132] With their transnational agendas,

---

[129] Tayfun, 2010.

[130] Tayfun, "Ethnicity Within Ethnicity" Among Turkish Speaking Immigrants in London.

[131] Ibid.

[132] Ansari, *The Infidel Within*, 366.

some Turkish associations have contributed to the rise of identity politics, for example the followers of Süleyman Hilmi Tunahan and *Milli Görüş* (National Vision), who generally focus on political grievances whether external (the Palestine and Kashmir causes for instance) or internal (anti-religious-discrimination law and the Salman Rushdie affair). This trend has further institutionalized ideas of Muslim unity—*ummah, da'wa/tebligh* (the call to Islam and preaching with the purpose of converting non-Muslims to Islam), and the preservation of faith and Islamic identity[133]—while remaining silent on the internal grievances of inter-ethnic cleavages and the desperate socio-economic status of the Muslim Turkish community. These concerns have placed mounting pressures on the second generation, which is largely suspended between three dominant spheres of cultural identity—British society, Muslim identity, and the Turkish background—which have contentious and, at best, controversial political and historical resonance.[134] Surrounded by associations that passively extend national mainland models of Islamism and place ultimate emphasis on political and transnational causes, the second generation of the various Turkish communities faced an integration crisis that urgently required an intellectual and organizational accommodation of their needs, especially the need for a model of "healthy integration."

The severity of such concerns is examined in a recent government report[135] that explains their influence on the current map of ethno-political, religious, and cultural divergences within the Turkish community, highlighting factors such as (1) their different position *vis-à-vis* their parents, the youth having been educated and socialized within British society and with relatively poor knowledge of their mother tongue; (2) their parents' preoccupation with economic sustenance activities, leading to a "generational deafness"; (3) a socialization crisis due to the lack of educational achievement, unemployment, inter-ethnic violence, crime, and the spread of street-gang culture; and (4) the threat they

---

[133] Ibid., 360–366.

[134] See Küçükcan, *Politics of Ethnicity, Identity and Religion*, 113–143.

[135] Change Institute, The Turkish and Turkish Cypriot Muslim Community in England.

pose to ethnic markets by shifting their consumption habits toward mainstream and international markets.[136]

Moreover, some of the above-mentioned social and economic grievances are seriously exacerbated by what is termed "invisibility"[137]— the absence of accurate statistics about the Turkish community's real numbers and the lack of "cultural markers" compared to other minorities, Afro-Caribbean, for instance—and this invisibility has resulted in their neglect in public policies dealing with social and economic disadvantages.[138]

In this context, the Hizmet Movement emerged as an intellectual and organizational departure from the Muslim community's mainstream focus on national and international politics. Aiming for the "betterment of human life," it opened an avenue for social mobility through addressing socio-economic concerns: adequate education, integration, *temsil* (religion in practice) rather than *tebliğ* (preaching to non-Muslims), and dialogue and cooperation with British mainstream social, political, and economic forces for better articulation of the community needs. The dialogue and cooperation theme of its activism, beside education, media and business, gained greater attention from political and social actors following the 7/7 (2005) attacks, once the movement had worked actively on communicating its goals and achievements to society. This enabled the movement to have a stronger presence as a network of community-service organizations aiming at the elimination of ignorance, poverty, and internal schism. The last in this list seemed to clearly articulate the renewed Muslim–non-Muslim divide in the society. These "enemies" were also seen by movement participants as main reasons for the penetration of extremist religious beliefs. In a

---

[136] Enneli et al, *Young Turks and Kurds: A Set of "Invisible" Disadvantaged Groups*; Change Institute, The Turkish and Turkish Cypriot Muslim Community in England; Tayfun, "Ethnicity Within Ethnicity" Among Turkish Speaking Immigrants in London; Cilingir, Identity and Integration among Turkish Sunni Muslims in Britain.

[137] Enneli et al, *Young Turks and Kurds: A Set of "Invisible" Disadvantaged Groups*; Thomson et al, *"Turks" in London: Shades of Invisibility and the Shifting Relevance of Policy in the Migration Process*.

[138] Mehmet Ali, *Turkish Speaking Communities and Education*, 87.

video release by the Dialogue Society, "Peace Through Education and Dialogue" the movement examines the causes of violent extremism committed by people professing to be of religion. In an interview with Nuriye Akman which was published in Zaman in 2004, Gülen pointed to the lack of education in Islam as one of the reasons some were deluded into joining terrorist organizations and projects.

In this way, the mobilizing factors for the Hizmet Movement developed through manifesting its purpose, objectives, and its strong faith-based collective identity. It developed in two parallel and intersecting domains: the local *sohbet*s (friendship circles) throughout the 1990s, and the organizational momentum toward the end of the 1990s.

The evolution of Hizmet in London

The 1990s witnessed a transnational diffusion of the Hizmet Movement as a large-scale community service movement. During this decade it became particularly responsive to local demands, mainly through its threefold strategy: firstly, its "glocal" themes of activism—thinking globally and acting locally; secondly, its internal composition of occupational groups, characterized by many attributes of a profession (educational requirements for certification, an ethic of community service, a base of knowledge and skills, training internships) and domination of leading occupational positions within the movement organizations by social science majors in intercultural and inter-faith dialogue activities; and finally, its bureaucratic elements that fostered the manifestation of developing career lines, routinization of leadership, accounting systems and division of labor. Such characteristics spoke well to the need in London to enhance the educational achievements of Turkish youth, enhance their employment opportunities and develop the skills and qualities of collective action and good models of integration. With these qualities it allowed for continuity between individual and collective aspirations. Growing evidence, explained in later sections, indicates the movement's success in mobilizing moral, organizational, human and material resources.

The local circles level of the Hizmet Movement

During the 1990s, local circles (*sohbets*) were organized around the ideas of Gülen, who visited the United Kingdom in 1993 and inspired many local groups to follow his approach to community service. Consequently, in 1994 an educational trust was established and *The Fountain* magazine was launched in London, beside many other charitable projects: supplementary schools, religious concerts, neighborhood outreach, and so on.

As described by a teacher participant, the Hizmet local circles that were initiated then and spread thereafter comprised two types of participant: firstly, academics, students, businessmen and intellectuals who had migrated from Turkey in the 1980s and early 1990s; and secondly, members of the working and lower middle classes, who had migrated from the central and the north-eastern and Black Sea provinces of Turkey, known for their poor educational and general infrastructure. The socio-economic composition of the Hizmet Movement in London was greatly affected by the ethno-cultural qualities of the latter group that dominates what McAdam (1988) terms the "demand side" for resource mobilization.

Although McAdam's approach pays little attention to purposeful and solidary incentives for collective action, it points to the main factors and constraints that shaped the socio-economic composition of the Hizmet Movement in London. As described by a leader in the Mevlana Rumi Mosque, these factors include (1) the large numbers of Cypriot Turks who generally show less interest in faith-based community service; (2) the momentous rise in the number of Kurdish immigrants in the 1990s; (3) the rise in the number of Kurdish immigrants supportive of the Kurdistan Workers' party (PKK)[139] or its separatist ideology; (4) the relatively small number of Turkish community members in the United Kingdom (approximately 80,000)[140] compared to

---

[139] A listed terrorist organization founded by Abdullah Öcalan in 1978. It aims to establish the state of Kurdistan in northern Iraq and southeastern Turkey through the use of violence.

[140] Change Institute, The Turkish and Turkish Cypriot Muslim Community in England, 27.

4.5 million Turks and German citizens of Turkish background in Germany[141]; (5) the socio-economic composition of Turkish minorities in the United Kingdom (rural and low educational background, with ultimate focus placed on economic survival, yet with a general Sunni and cultural background supportive of faith-based community service); (6) the high cost of obtaining land ownership and opening private schools, hospitals and health care centers in the United Kingdom; (7) the relatively recent arrival of Turkish minorities in the United Kingdom, among whom second-generation concerns have only lately appeared; and (8) the relatively weak role of the Turkish Directorate of Religious Affairs mosques that contribute to the immigration of qualified religious clerics, whether from Hizmet or other religious groups.

Concerning their prior acquaintance with the Hizmet Movement, some participants had already attended Gülen sermons prior to their arrival in the United Kingdom, while others only heard of him through their social networks in London. In both cases, a large proportion of Hizmet supporters consisted of Turkish mainland immigrants in the 1990s. It also follows that the Hizmet circles have been geographically concentrated in north London until the dispersion of the Turkish community began to occur in recent decades. A bloc recruitment model of mobilization is facilitated through the existing family and kinship relationships that underlie the community as well as the preceding organizational forms of collective action in the Turkish communities. With new Turkish communities being established in different parts of London (as well as other cities in the United Kingdom), the Hizmet circles also began to spread.

As mentioned earlier, a local circle is affectionately called a *"sohbet"* and is organized around a set of themes, such as brotherhood, fear of God or piety (*takva*), self-sacrifice, and so on. While the religious content is usually the most important part, socializing, entertainment, and discussing daily life make up the rest of a *sohbet* occasion.

---

[141] These statistics are drawn from the German census in 2005, and Woellert, Kroehnert et al., 2009. Both are cited in Karcher, Integrating Turks in Germany, 7.

My participant observations indicated that the substantive, organizational, spatial, and participation characteristics of *sohbet*s develop new spaces and rules for socialization and communicative activity. In *sohbet*s, the social relations of ordinary Turkish participants are diversified to include the neighborhood, associates in projects and friends of different backgrounds. While these networks may develop over weekly *sohbet*s, seasonal and project-oriented *sohbet*s strengthen social and economic ties and contribute to transnational networking for project initiatives.

The organizational level of the Hizmet Movement

The development of the Hizmet Movement in London during the 1990s resembled that of Hizmet in its early years in Turkey, when many of its supporters belonged to groups of local and small tradesmen. The focus in London in the early days was placed on various community service projects: collective dinners, neighborhood days and food or book fairs (*kermes*), as described by a Mevlana Rumi Mosque participant. The spread of local circles among professional groups—academics, artists, journalists, students, and businessmen—led to the development of previously *ad hoc* and mostly seasonal charitable projects into organizations where decision making is institutionalized around resolute and clear goals, by which the movement's centrifugal forces were mitigated to their minimum.

The organizational momentum of Hizmet activities relies on achieving the utmost social and economic utility of Hizmet participants. There is no central funding: participants run projects with independent financial, human, and socio-organizational resources. This diffusion mechanism supports a norm of micro-leadership in each organization, where creativity, innovation and self-fulfillment of participants contribute to the efficient use of resources.[142] As Oberschall concludes, "the greater the number of organizations in a collectivity, and the

---

[142] In this study, the term 'diffusion mechanism' refers to the "cognitive process (which) facilitates the dissemination of ideas and models that cause actors to perceive new possibilities or imperatives for action." Strang and Meyer (1993) in Campbell, Where Do We Stand?, 53.

higher the participation of members in that network, the more rapidly and enduringly does the mobilization (…) occur."[143]

In the first decade of the twenty-first century, a number of organizations emerged independently realizing Hizmet's principles: Axis Educational Trust was founded in 1994; the Dialogue Society was founded in 1999; the Stamford Hill Supplementary School ran from 2001 to 2007; Oxford Vision started delivering English language courses in 2003; the Anatolian Muslim Society has been running since 2004; the Mevlana Rumi Mosque was founded in 2008; and the BizNet magazine and business association, and academic groups for social research have been active since 2004.

Hizmet Movement efforts to integrate Turkish youth into British society started in the 1990s. Later, in the aftermath of the 7/7 (2005) attacks, one of the movement's more notable projects was the Friday sermon project, among eight initiatives presented in the Dialogue Society's policy reflection paper "Deradicalization by Default: The Dialogue Approach to Rooting Out Violent Extremism." In this paper the movement was critical of the Labour government's Prevent strategy. The Friday sermon project was launched to empower a moderate religious discourse in universities, mosques and workplaces: mosque sermons were prepared by Hizmet Movement participants and the texts offered free on the Internet.[144]

By the new millennium, Hizmet participants had grown in numbers and developed new aspirations and organizational structures: there was a need to institutionalize and systemize the efforts toward finding a shared ground, not only for various Turkish-speaking minorities, but also for the British and Muslim communities in general. The next section will examine two of the most important and active organizations of the Hizmet Movement in London, with due focus on their pattern of resource mobilization, as understood within the political, social, and economic contexts of Turkish, and more generally Muslim, communities in London.

---

[143] Oberschall, *Social Conflict and Social Movements*, 125.
[144] State funding was received for this project.

The Dialogue Society

The Dialogue Society was initiated by a number of Turkish and British–Turkish community activists in London who had been inspired by Gülen's sermons during the 1994–1996 period, in which he focused on dialogue and tolerance as crucial values in the development of a Muslim identity in modern times. The Dialogue Society describes itself in the following terms:

> The Dialogue Society is a registered charity, established in London in 1999, with the aim of advancing social cohesion by connecting communities, empowering people to engage and contributing to the development of ideas on dialogue and community building. It does this by bringing people together through discussion forums, courses, capacity building, publications and outreach. It operates nationwide with regional branches across the UK. It was founded by British Muslims of Turkish background inspired by the teachings and example of Muslim scholar and peace activist Fethullah Gülen. The Dialogue Society is not a religious or ethnic organization. It aims to facilitate dialogue on a whole range of social issues, regardless of any particular faith or religion. It stands for democracy, human rights, the non-instrumentalization of religion in politics, equality and freedom of speech.

In addition, the successful initiative of the Journalists and Writers Foundation (JWF) in Turkey awakened a sense of communal and social responsibility in Hizmet participants in the United Kingdom, according to a Dialogue Society leader. The main values advocated by Gülen, and also represented in the Dialogue Society, are "respect for diversity, equal access to human rights and freedom of thought, the rule of law and loyalty to the law of the land, proactive citizenship and democratic engagement and the non-instrumentalization of religion in politics."[145]

Between 1999 and 2006 the Dialogue Society focused solely on community based projects and on cultivating social constituencies through charitable initiatives: organizing Whirling Dervish concerts, communal fast-breaking (*iftar*) Friendship Dinners during Ramadan,

---

[145] www.dialoguesociety.org.

community conferences around days of religious importance, inter-faith picnics and fairs, and small group discussions with local police forces and authorities. During this period its first large-scale event was a Dinner and Award Ceremony at the House of Lords. As stated by its Executive Director, these events sought to mobilize first- and sec-ond-generation British Muslim communities and facilitate their exchange with and understanding of different cultures and faiths. Although they were successful in mobilizing social and communal support, these activ-ities, he maintains, were *ad hoc*, seasonal and volunteer-based.

In 2007, a three-day international conference on the movement was held in London. On the momentum the conference generated, various perspectives and initiatives were introduced for an organized, systematic and effectively structured plan of dialogue-related commu-nity service; the Dialogue Society rented its first offices in 2008 and began complementing its community work with academic outreach and projects.

Due to the substantive contribution of academics, activists and intellectuals to shaping the idea of the Dialogue Society, an advisory board was established to share the Dialogue Society's strategic plan-ning and decision-making processes. Through their annual meetings, email, and face-to-face communication, advisors' opinions, varied exper-tise, and knowledge are systematically delivered to the Dialogue Soci-ety team, which potentially multiplies its outreach through its advisors' "overlapping affiliations."[146] Moreover, the Dialogue Society organized school tours for students of various backgrounds and collaborated with a number of organizations through specialized workshops and seminars.

The Mevlana Rumi Mosque

The Mevlana Rumi Mosque was founded in 2008 by the Anatolian Muslim Society—a registered charity established in 2004 by British Muslims of Turkish background. According to one of its leaders, the Mevlana Rumi Mosque was primarily established in response to local needs, which were closely aligned with Anatolian Muslim Society goals;

---

[146] Diani, *Networks and Participation*, 348.

one of its goals—as stated in a promotional leaflet—is "to promote (…) community cohesion in the United Kingdom," especially among Turks from different ethnic backgrounds.

As a mosque and community centre, its primary target audience is Muslims in North London; as a community centre providing faith neutral public talks and services, its secondary target audience appears to be communities living, working and studying locally to Edmonton. The mosque provides a religious and spiritual environment, resources, and instruction in Turkish and English that assist in developing a moderate model of Muslimhood in the neighboring area. Friday sermons are delivered in Turkish and English at equal length, and some projects assist Muslims to learn about religious duties such as daily prayers and Ramadan fasting. Also, socialization and supplementary classes for students enable the mosque to provide a role model for Muslim youth in the face of a number of social challenges: crime, racial tension, isolation and violence.

While the Mevlana Rumi Mosque is still at an early stage of development, the Dialogue Society has reached a stage of maturity,[147] and even elaboration and structure, with its new professional and chapter-based type of community service. The development of both organizations, however, illustrates Oberschall's theory[148] of mobilization in which the two conditions she sets are present: firstly, the pre-existence of an organizational base and leadership (present in the Hizmet Movement local circles), and secondly, a segmented society that permits, nevertheless, a certain degree of mobility and exchange among its stratified groups—a factor also present in the Turkish community's case in London.

---

[147] This point draws upon Schmid's classification of an organization's life-cycles in which organizations start with formation/entrepreneurial, development/collectivity, maturation/formalization, elaboration and structure, then decline and stagnation (Schmid, *Leadership Styles and Leadership Change in Human and Community Service Organization*, 403).

[148] Oberschall, *Social Conflict and Social Movements,* 1993.

The supply side: Micro-mobilization

In this study a Social Movement Organization (SMO) is defined as "a complex formal organization which identifies its goals with the preferences of a social movement (…) and attempts to implement these goals."[149] Hunt and Benford identify the "micro-mobilization" processes of SMOs as "the collaborative work individuals do on behalf of a social movement or social movement organization to muster, ready, coordinate, use, and reproduce material resources, labor, and ideas for collective action."[150] This takes place through supplying participants and potential organizational cadres with different opportunities for participation. In this regard, the Dialogue Society and Mevlana Rumi Mosque "supply" can be classified under the following headings:

1. *Community cohesion*: The Dialogue Society arranges conferences and colloquiums, panel discussions and workshops that usually attract academics, journalists, professionals, students, and community leaders. In addition, it undertakes outreach initiatives for community organizations, policy-makers, and universities. On the Mevlana Rumi Mosque side, interfaith events, school visits, summer and vacation camps usually attract neighboring families and children.

2. *Capacity building*: Since 2006, the Dialogue Society has focused on capacity building of individuals, social groups and organizations, through providing consultancy and coaching services, publications, access to public discussions and seminars, along with skill-based programs, dialogue, media, and success schools.

3. *Educational support*: The Mevlana Rumi Mosque provides a number of educational services: Qur'an lessons, Turkish language courses, music, culture and morals courses; for parents, a number of *sohbet*s take place during their children's class time.

4. *Religious services*: Among the Mevlana Rumi Mosque primary activities is the provision of fixed courses, *sohbet*s, and sermons: the mosque functions as a worship facility where services such as marriages, religious consultation, and funerals are provided.

---

[149] McCarthy and Zald, Resource Mobilization and Social Movements, 1217–8.
[150] Hunt and Benford, Collective Identity, Solidarity and Commitment, 438.

Conclusion

SMO theorists see the likelihood that activists will combine one or two forms of activism as related to the amount of time and effort required.[151] Moreover, organizational strategies usually involve an understanding of the combination of activity forms that the SMO offers, based on its philosophy and pool of resources, and also based on the demand side; namely, what target participants can aim for. While the Dialogue Society depends on the purposeful participation of its constituencies—students, activists, academics and organizations—the Mevlana Rumi Mosque relies on more informal types of participation; for example, housewives are invited to participate in activities while their children are at school and their husbands—often local businessmen or traders—are at work.

The wide variety of activities offered by both the Dialogue Society and the Mevlana Rumi Mosque reflects the Hizmet Movement's inclusive approach to community service, through which participants and beneficiaries are offered opportunities that develop their potential and that demand more contribution on their part. Overlapping activities are also explained through both organizations' dependence on coinciding social constituencies. While the more recent launch of the Mevlana Rumi Mosque and its dependence on beneficiary constituencies explains its *ad hoc* and seasonal type of activism, the Dialogue Society in contrast, has institutionalized its community service and shifted its focus toward capacity building.

---

[151] McCarthy and Zald, The Enduring Vitality of the Resource Mobilization Theory of Social Movements, 542.

CHAPTER 4

Hizmet's Know-how

In his study of social movement organizations, Lofland mirrors Zald and Ash's (1966) dichotomy of inclusive and exclusive SMOs, by detailing possible structures of SMOs in terms of their scope of involvement in five types of forms. Among these are associations sustained by volunteers and collectives comprised of cooperating workers.[152]

The Dialogue Society local and national chapters focus on "(i) supporting local communities and stakeholders[153] and (ii) capacity building through partnerships, consultancy, training, publications and advocacy."[154] Its participants (whether full-time or part-time, paid or not) have settled job descriptions, while volunteers provide task-based technical services, such media and IT assistance. In comparison, Mevlana Rumi Mosque is a loosely structured local facility overseen by a board of trustees, with a task-oriented structure collectively served by volunteering and unpaid teachers and administrators.

Organizational structure, functions, and rules

While the Mevlana Rumi Mosque volunteers share a relatively homogeneous Turkish background, the Dialogue Society cadre represents a

---

[152] Lofland in McAdam et al. Social Movements, 717. Many studies of such SMOs informed my research—mainly Gamson, *The Strategy of Social Protest*; Kanter, *Commitment and Community*; Curtis and Louise A. Zurcher, Stable Resources of Protest Movement.

[153] The Fellowship Dialogue Society and Education and Dialogue Charity emerged through this effort.

[154] www.dialoguesociety.org.

wider array of identities, cutting across ethnicities, religions, professional backgrounds,[155] and cultures. Standard criteria for participation include good academic research skills and past experience in office work and dialogue activities. Similarly, the Mevlana Rumi Mosque applies a number of tools to ensure maximum effectiveness of its work: courses are assigned according to specialized background, past experience in teaching, and very good communication and administrative skills. Presentation, negotiation and office working skills, as well as observance of the rules of discipline are also required, and participants must provide a certificate from the Criminal Records Bureau to be eligible to teach. To encourage qualified teachers to volunteer, childcare services are offered.

Both the Mevlana Rumi Mosque and the Dialogue Society recruit participants through various means such as internships, word of mouth, and social networks such as kinship and neighborhood networks. However, some Dialogue Society participants learned about it through occupational networks. Whatever the recruitment source, training, support, and skill-based courses are offered to enhance participants' career skills. A Dialogue Society project coordinator said, *"It is intellectually stimulating. The work they do is important, well thought of. I have learnt a lot in the last few months. I'm raising my competence in many skills related to my career."* Another Dialogue Society participant emphasized, *"Although I am not a good public speaker, the Dialogue Society pushes my potentials to their utmost utility."*

Mevlana Rumi Mosque teachers are supported through seminars and workshops, monthly sessions for curriculum planning, and consultation (*istişare*) with teachers at other Hizmet organizations. Teaching by experience, especially in religious festivals, by example (*temsil*) and by offering moral rewards is in the range of methods applied in Mevlana Rumi Mosque classes.

The organizations' "internal system"[156] is further institutionalized through formal and informal rules. While the Dialogue Society applies

---

[155] Graduates are usually qualified in social sciences, though some branches recruit participants from other specializations.

[156] Melucci, *Challenging Codes*, 315.

formally documented regulations regarding decision making, problem solving, coordination and communication, the Mevlana Rumi Mosque's loose and vulnerable hierarchy[157] applies "oral laws"[158] to ensure professionalism, sustainability, and good interpersonal relations within and outside the charity. Although volunteers demonstrate a professional attitude to their work, the Mevlana Rumi Mosque has still to formalize work procedures and external communication policies.

"Professional SMOs" are identified as possessing specific qualities, such as devoted full-time leadership, resources drawn from conscience groups, and small teams of professional cadres that focus on potential constituencies.[159] The Dialogue Society aims to transform its activity to become academically constituted, with clear career forms, traineeships and hierarchies of academic and practical expertise and skill; it will co-organize a Master of Arts program in Dialogue Studies, through which it aims to become an action-oriented think tank, where both academia and practical expertise are interdependently developed.

In its turn, to ensure long-term effectiveness and sustainability, the Mevlana Rumi Mosque deploys certain techniques: engaging parents in *sohbets*, sustaining one-to-one teaching by example, and developing communication and leadership skills through camps and competitions that mosque leaders hope will produce future leaders of teachers and students. At the time of my research, twenty of nearly 270 students attending the mosques on weekends are regularly integrated in class-related activities; that is, they lead classes, organize students, help in instructing and training, exams and quizzes, and other such activities. These "role-model" students realize qualities highly encouraged by the Mevlana Rumi Mosque teachers: good acquaintance with basic religious knowledge; good Qur'an reading skills; and observance of culturally encouraged codes of behavior, such as offering refreshments

---

[157] An adjustable structure in which each participant's authority and responsibility expand and shrink on goal-related bases.

[158] Schmid, Leadership Styles and Leadership Change in Human and Community Service Organization, 404.

[159] McCarthy and Zald, *The Trend of Social Movements in America*.

to visitors, and using polite, formal terms of address for their elders, or to introduce or apologize.

During work time, participants in both organizations present norms of flexibility, commitment, sacrifice, and hospitality. A Dialogue Society participant said, *"You do not know which thing you do is the most pleasing to God. In the Dialogue Society you may get involved in tasks such as greeting guests, giving public speeches, networking with organizations. You may also roll up your sleeves and prepare food in the kitchen, clean bathrooms, and meet politicians."* Another example is the Dialogue Society academic director, who designs and coordinates seminars, while a volunteer is pressing tablecloths and dishwashing. None of the Dialogue Society participants ask for overtime compensation, although they might be recruited on a part-time or part-paid basis. Within a similar familial and informal environment, Mevlana Rumi Mosque volunteers interchange most of their tasks in an immensely flexible manner.

These norms indicate the organizations' social capital of legitimacy and trust.[160] Participants in the Dialogue Society and Mevlana Rumi Mosque cadres demonstrate a strong ideational commitment to the goals and values nurtured through Gülen's writings. In this way, incentives within the organizations are mainly symbolic, normative and value-based. The main values and norms I found represented in both organizations were altruism, negotiation, honor and dignity, dialogue and consultation (*istişare*), and tolerance toward difference.

Among the rules observed within both the Dialogue Society and Mevlana Rumi Mosque is, firstly, collective accountability; since responsibilities are duplicated among cadre members, it encourages collective and consensual decision making according to the movement's tradition of consultation (*istişare*) and results in a rising *esprit de corps*.[161] This enables different patterns of "functional leadership" to emerge: professional (e.g., the Dialogue Society media director), expertise-based

---

[160] A number of approaches attempt to explain this phenomenon in SMOs: Lofland, *Social Movement Organizations*,197–225, Melucci, *Challenging Codes*, 318–327, and Edwards and McCarthy, Resources and Social Movement Organization, 120.

[161] Bass and Avolio 1990 in Schmid, Leadership Styles and Leadership Change in Human and Community Service Organization, 402.

(e.g., a Mevlana Rumi Mosque teacher), and articulation leadership (e.g. the Dialogue Society Executive Director and a Mevlana Rumi Mosque secretary).

Secondly, it follows that the possibility that leaders might exploit their position, authority, information, or resources for their own benefit is mitigated by the way in which "everyone is accountable to everyone," which resonates with Skocpol's note about the inclusive form of decision making in grassroots SMOs.[162]

Furthermore, new project leaders are supported with material, technical, and financial resources in order to ensure a successful start. This rule is also relevant to self-fulfillment within Hizmet organizations. As noted by a Dialogue Society member, individuals have access to the resources and services of the organization by which they can realize their ideas. This nurtures qualities such as social trust, honesty, flexibility, adaptability and immediacy.[163] Moreover, it results in the stable and enduring participation of members, as in the Dialogue Society case, where, unless pressured by unexpected financial responsibilities in their private lives, individuals are not projecting any departure from their workplace and practices.

In addition, a progressive self re-structuring of each organization takes place in order to fill the gap between participants' performance and the organization's expectations. For instance, the flexible structure of the Mevlana Rumi Mosque results in adopting mutable goals with negotiated mechanisms, as in the case of transforming its initial target from opening a supplementary school to opening a mosque, based on local participants' demand.[164]

Finally, a rule of zero entry and exit cost[165] allows for negotiating individual ambitions and collective goals. In the long run, volunteers may pursue self-development through different projects. New volunteers usually take over earlier projects. In every case, collective respon-

---

[162] Skocpol, *Diminished Democracy*.

[163] Özdalga, Redeemer or Outsider?, 434.

[164] Source: A Mevlana Rumi Mosque leader, March 2011.

[165] That is, individuals may freely join with other participants to work on a project and freely leave again according to their availability and circumstances.

sibility and accountability facilitate the continuation of projects after the departure of individual volunteers.

This norm of functional leadership, however, does not suggest an absence of strong organizational identity. The work of each member in the professional cadre represents a continuing process of construction and reconstruction of the organizations' collective identity. This point is expanded in the following paragraphs.

Many historical and cultural metaphors support Gülen's view of non-denominational dialogue among human beings and hence represent both organizations' *raison d'être*. Among the references that are often used by the Dialogue Society to expand upon this point are: (1) the poet Yunus Emre's line, "We love the created because of the Creator"; (2) Mevlana Rumi's famous call "Come!"[166]; and (3) Gülen's advice: "Open your heart, become wide like the ocean. Let there be no troubled souls to whom you do not offer a hand and about whom you remain unconcerned."[167]

Accordingly, the main values that thematically unite the different identities of participants and their activities include tolerance, humanism, forgiveness, responsibility, and consciousness of one's community. While some participants only heard of Hizmet and Gülen after starting their work or activism, participants expressed a range of values that hold them committed to Hizmet: respect for difference, professionalism, openness toward different cultures, consistency of personal and professional values, and creativity. Moreover, a strong sense of collective identity, cultivated through Gülen's teachings, results in a sense of ownership. As one Mevlana Rumi Mosque teacher quoted a Muslim convert saying, "How lucky I am—I have a whole mosque as my home!"

Zald and McCarthy maintain that demand and commitment increase as the SMO meets the expected needs of the population where it func-

---

[166] "Come, come, come again/Whoever you may be/Come again, even though/You be a pagan or fire worshipper/Ours is not the threshold of despair/Come again, even if you have/Violated your vows a hundred times/Come again…". Rumi.

[167] The Dialogue Society official website, accessed on April 2011.

tions[168]: the Mevlana Rumi Mosque's manager asserts that "if we open another mosque two hundred meters away, people will fill it and still feel they need another social utility like it."

Participation and relationships

The Dialogue Society applies a wide diffusion strategy as it strives to broaden and maintain its community roots. It coordinates its initiatives and projects with three main sectors—community, academia, and media.[169] It also maintains its relations with stakeholders and policy makers through informing them about its work, offering consultation, and organizing round-table discussions. Its audience consists of intellectuals, academics, social activists, students of different backgrounds, community representatives and politicians. University students generally populate skill-based courses.[170] Moreover, through inter-organizational networks, the Dialogue Society is able to mobilize professional volunteers from the organization in dialogue-related activism, for example, its project coordinator at the time of my research.

On the Mevlana Rumi Mosque side, Turkish, Cypriot and Kurdish students attend classes while their parents are approached to attend *sohbet*s organized around topics such as fraternity,[171] community, and sincerity.[172] Information-based *sohbet*s for new converts are held on a weekly basis, to avoid giving *ad hoc* answers to enquirers. These *soh-*

---

[168] McCarthy and Zald, The Enduring Vitality of the Resource Mobilization Theory of Social Movements, 535.

[169] Kalyoncu illustrates the diffusion of Gülen's ideas through direct inter-personal relations with bureaucrats, civil servants, clerics and businessmen. According to him, this builds up a sense of trust, especially with local authorities that are "introduced to the movement even before they start investigating its activity." *A Civilian Response to Ethno-Religious Conflict*, 16–8.

[170] The Hizmet Movement's diffusion strategy focuses on student networks, through which prior contacts are varied, easily developed and sustainable over time. Moreover, 'prior contact' (interpersonal relations) is proved to be the strongest, most robust, factor in almost every study on Social Movements, e.g., Gerlach and Hine, *People, Power, Change*; Heirich, *Change of Heart*; McAdam 1986 cited in McAdam et al. Social Movements.

[171] Participant observation (06/03/2011).

[172] Participant observation (03/04/11).

*bet*s include discussion of the basics of Islamic faith and common issues among faiths, such as the lives of Joseph and Moses.

Participation, according to Zald and McCarthy, is a normal behavior that does not necessarily emerge out of "personal alienation (but rather) of biographical circumstances, social supports, and immediate life situations."[173] During my stay at the Mevlana Rumi Mosque, I encountered two interesting examples of parent participants. The first was a middle-aged woman who had started volunteering ten years earlier after her husband's death—an event that had urged communal support from the Turkish neighborhood. The other was a parent who commuted two hours every weekend to bring her children to classes that, in her view, preserved their identity and faith while developing solid bases for their integration: "We could not manage it, so let these people do it," she said.

The social networking between participants and potential participants is necessary for raising demand for participation.[174] In addition, successful SMOs are those who depend on "conscience constituencies"[175] rather than beneficiary ones. As far as can be observed, the Mevlana Rumi Mosque widens its conscience constituencies firstly through encouraging participants to hold local *sohbet*s in work places, shops, restaurants, houses and during social events. As one teacher explained, *"We go to people and call them to visit our mosque; we do not wait for them to find us."*[176] In these *sohbet*s participants discuss daily-life issues, narrate sacrifices of the Prophet's companions and other Hizmet Movement participants, and encourage moral reward, for example, through

---

[173] McCarthy and Zald, The Enduring Vitality of the Resource Mobilization Theory of Social Movements, 535.

[174] Ibid. 543.

[175] Conscience constituencies: those who believe in the rightness of a cause, even if they themselves, their relatives or friends will not directly benefit from the cause of the movement (Ibid., 536).

[176] *Hizmet* organizations in this regard contribute to the accumulation of social capital, which Putnam defines as "connections among individuals—social networks and norms of reciprocity and trustworthiness that arise from them." *Bowling Alone*, 19. Weller also notes that faith-based community service "contributes significantly to the preservation and development of both bonding and bridging social capital." Religions and Social Capital, 272.

selling books about Hizmet's core concepts or Gülen's teachings. Secondly, the Mevlana Rumi Mosque acquires local media coverage, usually by local Turkish media such as the Zaman Britanya and Zaman Weekly and other local Turkish newspapers; and thirdly, it enables communal gatherings and discussions in its socialization area.

*Sohbet*s are held along location, profession, gender, and project lines, where "insiders and outsiders are almost indistinguishable,"[177] since different levels of mobilization are integrated. By reinforcing inter-communal relations, and relations with the Turkish community, as well as the wider society, a fast flow of information is realized as Hizmet organizations communicate their needs and offer their assistance to other projects within *sohbet*s.

An important remark must be made here about the movement's stance on women's activism. A general strength of the Hizmet Movement is that a great many female participants are, as I observed, university graduates, and many of them pursue their careers in relevant workplaces. They openly interact and socialize within study and/or work environments. There is a general tendency for women to become teachers in various educational establishments. The movement also empowers single female students from rural and culturally conservative regions of Turkey to pursue their studies internationally through applying for universities where Hizmet-managed student dorms are available. In this way, the Hizmet Movement provides possibilities for female participants to realize their potential to varying degrees; this depends on a set of biographical and structural determinants: their age, marital status, education, level of consciousness and general knowledge, past experiences, career prospects, along with the political, cultural, and socio-economic determinants of the place where they serve.

In this regard, religiously motivated head-covering for women is generally among the most controversial issues.[178] Hizmet participants are generally advised that they are not to blame if they must remove their headscarf to pursue their education and careers. Thus, adequate

---

[177] Melucci, *Challenging Codes*, 309.

[178] See for instance the writer's treatment of this issue in Yavuz, *Islamic Political Identity in Turkey*, 99.

education and service to humanity is prioritized over the sense of personal piety reflected in wearing the headscarf. Whether they had decided to keep or take off their headscarf, women encountered in this study were found to be strongly committed to living religious lives and achieving the Hizmet goals of serving society. Meanwhile, whenever possible, women are encouraged to pursue their education and hold career positions for which they qualify, either within or outside Hizmet organizations. In this regard, the Hizmet Movement is qualitatively different from Islamic movements for which women's head covering is an essential aspect of identity politics. Some cases I encountered in Turkey in 2009 also indicated that the movement's flexible stance on this matter was a major reason for people from other Islamic movements deciding to switch or extend their affiliations and participate in Hizmet.

Material and financial resources

Though financially independent of each other, both the Dialogue Society and the Mevlana Rumi Mosque raise funds through sympathetic local businessmen and professionals, mainly from those of a Turkish background. The movement reached out to them in the 1990s through *sohbet*s and charity projects. One example of these supporters is an extremely successful Turkish–British businessman who first became acquainted with the Hizmet Movement in 1993 through his wife's social networks; this acquaintance later developed into a *sohbet* relationship. When asked about his motive for contributing more than ten percent of his yearly income, he referred to the transparency of audits and financial records, honesty, innovation, and the non-misleading qualities of Hizmet organizations. He also maintained that through his financial contribution, a set of fundamental problems, such as poverty and ignorance, are considerably ameliorated. For him, therefore, observing the immediate and far-reaching results of Hizmet charities is a motivating factor.

Both organizations also solicit project-based state funds when possible. For instance, the Dialogue Society received funding from the Community and Local Governments Department for developing new resources to promote dialogue among communities, through publications and training projects. The Mevlana Rumi Mosque also sought government funding for renovating its historic building and providing classroom equipment.

Other sources of financial support are solicited through the Dialogue Society academic and professional networks. At the date of this study, the Dialogue Society was managing its budget according to a provisional estimate of yearly donations. For the future, new techniques to realize systematic and stable funding of the organization were being thoroughly studied, including distributing charity boxes (in which small donations on a monthly/weekly basis are collected), annual fundraising events, an application for Gift Aid,[179] project-based fundraising, and maximizing benefits of fixed costs by, for example, hiring out spaces such as meeting rooms and hall space.

The Mevlana Rumi Mosque's less formal, more familial structure enables the mobilization of direct and small donations, as well as material and service contributions from local businessmen, which comprise almost eighty percent of the Mevlana Rumi Mosque's running costs. Categories of contribution include one or more of the following: time (*sohbet*s), effort (volunteering for classes), money, services (e.g., maintaining the heating, roof, etc.), soliciting support from participants in neighboring areas, and supporting the access of impoverished recipients to Mevlana Rumi Mosque services. In such ways, as one of the mosque teachers told me, indirect reciprocity develops among service providers and recipients through which anonymous channeling of resources maintains social status, the sincerity of providers, and the dignity of recipients.

While Turkish socio-religious culture supports the *vakıf* (charitable trust) tradition in general, a number of challenges restrict the Mevlana Rumi Mosque resources. For example, many of the successful Turkish businessmen of Cypriot background in London, manifest a

---

[179] Gift Aid is a UK government scheme which increases the value of donations to charities by allowing them to reclaim basic rate tax on gifts or donations.

norm of "cultural religiosity"[180]; the socio-economic infrastructure of the Turkish community in London does not support big donations; and local participants usually target economic sustenance rather than the cultural competence and educational achievement of their children. Finally, I observed that there is a general strategy for fundraising within the Hizmet organizations, that is, "Act first, find money next." Volunteerism is assumed to cultivate a sense of collective responsibility for and ownership of the projects, ideas, and their results. It inspires social and individual commitment to the sustainability and effectiveness of such projects.

Conclusion

As repeatedly affirmed by my informants, both levels of the Hizmet Movement's activism—the local/grass-roots and organizational levels—are institutionally, financially and legally independent of Gülen. The movement cultivates functional leaders through its diffused, multi-faceted and multi-layered structure. Those leaders' functions, expertise, seniority, and place of residence determine the type of projects to which they can contribute. In fact, both the Dialogue Society and the Mevlana Rumi Mosque demonstrate a situation in which grassroots and organizational mobilization are complementary, interdependent, and equally successful, which refutes claims that Social Movements are destined for "oligarchization" after they reach a peak in their development.[181]

A number of micro-structural factors explain the persistent participation in Hizmet organizations: membership in other organizations, history of prior activism, biographical availability, and the resonance between communal and societal needs and the movement's goals. Of these factors, history of prior activism has the strongest explanatory power. The Hizmet Movement is largely dependent on student, professional, neighborhood and similar inter-personal networks,

---

[180] Küçükcan, The politics of ethnicity, identity and religion among Turks in London, 145–67.

[181] See Michels, *Political Parties* and Weber, *Economy and Society*.

which are sustainable over a long time: the individual "invest(ment) in time, energy, relationships, as well as more tangible resources in pursuing activism, (exacerbates) the costs of exit from such lines of action (and therefore) encourage(s) continued adherence to the role."[182] Over time, individuals engage in durable relations such as marriage.

Thus, the Hizmet Movement comprises two broad levels of activism. While the local/grass roots level provides resources, at the organizational level these resources are managed through a condensed, yet equally diffused, non-hierarchical structure.[183] In this way Hizmet proves more of a "Social Movement community" than a strictly bureaucratic SMO, with "fluid boundaries, flexible leadership structures, and malleable division of labor."[184] This also explains why it is impossible to estimate the number of its participants.[185]

On both national and transnational levels, no umbrella organization coordinates the communication among organizations. A rough estimate has been made of the number of Hizmet organizations, which has reached approximately 1,000 schools in Turkey and the world, supported by seven to ten million participants.[186] As observed in the London case, organizations are scattered over a range of varied activities, goals, participant profiles, and institutional development. Through local circles, these organizations, enterprises, and charities come into and stay in touch with each other. They also exchange expertise, information, and resources through local *sohbets*, bringing a degree of homogeneity in their mobilization mechanisms.

Competition among organizations is based on motivation, rather than for purposes of differentiation. The two levels, local and organizational activism, are complementary in the way in which grass roots local circles provide the flow of resources that are processed and effi-

---

[182] McAdam et al. Social Movements, 709.

[183] Other studies of *Hizmet* also describe the movement as a loosely knit social network. See Leman, The Flexible and Multilayered Character of "Hizmet" (Social Service) Movement in Immigration, 82.

[184] Buechler, Women's Movements in the United States, 42.

[185] Ebaugh, *The Gülen Movement*, 4.

[186] Ibid.

ciently used through organizations. In this way, no single organization can claim to represent the Hizmet Movement, while each one covers the spectrum of Hizmet activities to various degrees. Organizations and enterprises collectively fulfill the vision of Hizmet in education, intercultural dialogue, media and business.

CHAPTER 5

A New Type of Social Movement

The previous chapter discussed aspects of the mobilization of resources by Hizmet organizations, focusing on themes such as services, levels and dimensions of participation, relationships and diffusion strategy, leadership, inter-organizational relations and finance. The fieldwork research on both organizations indicates a breadth of Hizmet activities, profound commitment and devotion on the part of volunteers, persistent support of conscience and beneficiary constituencies, effective functional leadership, and the use of social networks for mobilizing financial resources. While the Mevlana Rumi Mosque is still striving to afford its minimum needs, it undertakes projects that turn its limited space into a densely populated social facility to which some parents commute long distances from their residence areas. The success of the Dialogue Society is also remarkable, as indicated by its advisors' comments that credit qualities of honesty, openness, and commitment to long-lasting relationships to the organization.[187] By these findings the Hizmet organizations function in accordance with Melucci's triple criteria for an SMO's success: (1) the reliability and legitimacy of Gülen's influence; (2) the density and robustness of the formal and informal networks of belonging; and (3) the ability to restructure and adapt these networks to new situations, such as the challenge of religion-tainted extremism following 7/7 (2005).[188]

---

[187] The Dialogue Society, *Interview with Simon Robinson*, no date.
[188] Melucci, *Challenging Codes*, 376–7.

Hizmet's strategic adaptivism

My field study of the Dialogue Society and the Mevlana Rumi Mosque reveals a general theme of strategic adaptivism. There is a continuous process of adjusting the movement's discourse and mechanisms to new challenges and demands from the surrounding environment, internal and external. While the Hizmet Movement's responsiveness to contextual challenges, opportunities, and needs is clearly adaptive, it is also strategic in the sense that it rests on a holistic view of how to deal with the environment of philanthropic professional activism. In other words, it differs from pragmatism, opportunism, and relativism in that it is rooted in a profound school of Islamic thought, described by some recent scholars as the theory of *maqasid* (the ultimate purposes of Islam) and *maslaha* (public well being or interest), as explained in Chapter Two.

Strategic adaptivism is driven by the various organizational aspects reviewed in the previous chapter. It is applied in the mobilization of all types of resources: moral, socio-organizational, human, and material.

Moral resources

The Dialogue Society and Mevlana Rumi Mosque's vision and methods are maintained by keeping the balance between the different components of each organization's identity in a way that makes it a potential common ground for professional volunteers from different backgrounds. For instance, Muslimness, underlined in individuals' private lives, is a source of moral legitimacy that attracts both Turkish Cypriot and Kurdish community members to the movement. Similarly, Turkishness explains recruiting Turkic students with Central Asian backgrounds to participate intensively, compared to participants of non-Anatolian ethnic/national backgrounds. However, the movement attempts to mitigate the Anatolian majority in inter-cultural dialogue projects. Also, Anatolian Muslimhood is most obvious through the emphasis on behavioral and organizational decorum, and is at the same time integrated into public health rules and social codes of modern societies or table etiquette directions as taught to children, amongst other examples. In this way, the movement utilizes its multi-

faceted identity for wider outreach. While maintaining objective separation between the different threads of its identity, it highlights each of
them on a task basis where it has specific spatial, socio-economic and
cultural resonance.

Socio-organizational resources

Recognizing the "glocal" transformation in world societies, the movement endorses decentralized decision-making mechanisms[189]—loose
structures of parallel, overlapping, and dense networks of activism dis-
persed around education, culture, media, business, and interfaith dialogue. In this way, Hizmet develops careers for professional activism.
Observing individual biographies of participants in the Dialogue Society and Mevlana Rumi Mosque, I found such career advancement to
be among the motivations for sustained participation in activities.
The potential for accumulating knowledge, experience and skills, and
thus to realize social mobility, results in the movement becoming a pre-
ferred network for some of its participants. Meanwhile, on the organization's side, different aspects of social mobility (professional, academic and socio-economic) are fulfilled in two dimensions of diffusion—vertical and horizontal. While Hizmet organizations function in
both dimensions, they vary according to the "functional niche"[190] they
occupy and therefore the type of social mobility offered. In the horizontal dimension, in addition to their direct dialogue objective, the
activities of the Dialogue Society provide its beneficiaries with opportunities to network with leading academics, professionals, stakeholders and key figures, which may be seen as useful in advancing their
career prospects. In the vertical dimension, neighborhood, associational, kinship and *cemaat* networks develop local, middle class, and
blue collar participants' communication, leadership, negotiation, and
marketing skills, which results in greater upward socio-economic
mobility over time. In this way, the complementary and intertwining
roles of different Hizmet organizations accommodate the various

---

[189] See Chapter Two on the *istişare* tradition within the movement.
[190] McCarthy and Zald, The Enduring Vitality of the Resource Mobilization Theory of
Social Movements, 538.

objectives of participation and fulfill them in varying degrees at local, national, and transnational levels.

Fethullah Gülen's informal school, mentioned in Chapter One, runs for a three- to four-year term and is usually attended by fifteen to twenty participants who subsequently participate in the movement's organizations and enterprises in Turkey and around the world, and teach Islamic studies informally within the Hizmet circles.[191] In this way, Gülen's knowledge encircles different community networks, develops new forms of religious discourse and knowledge and adds a sense of "community" to the Hizmet Movement's transnational networks.

Hizmet organizations thus remain associated with the teachings of Gülen and ideationally connected to each other. Although Gülen's Hizmet philosophy is realized in similar organizational forms—educational trusts, business associations, media organs, and so on—the prioritization of these forms and of the movement's associated goals is bound to the contextual determinants of each society.

Human resources

The Hizmet Movement aims to maximize the social and economic utility of participants' capabilities and potentials. In this regard, participants are not asked to quit their prior or other relationships, interests, lifestyles, ambitions, and so on. Rather, they are advised on how to network potential constituencies within and outside the Hizmet Movement for further diffusion of their activism. Thus, self-realization becomes an added value to the collective mobilization of the movement's resources. In my research I found many indicators reflecting the extent of utilization of human resource capacities within the movement:

1) Conscience groups: those who hold positive views of the movement, based on media or observation sources, and may/may not be benefiting from its activities;

2) A high number of female participants of a variety of backgrounds and ages and in a variety of roles;

---

[191] Ibid.

3) Attendees of seminars, workshops, programs and mosque courses;

4) Attendees of larger sohbets, delivered by students of Gülen;

5) Attendees of smaller and often weekly neighborhood or profession-based sohbets;

6) Attendees of *himmet* meetings, where planning of projects and fundraising take place;

7) Attendees of *mütevelli* (board meetings, steering committee meetings);

8) Intellectuals and older members of the movement: writers about Gülen from the movement, and those who produce intellectual texts in the movement.

At the heart of this scaling[192] is that Hizmet as a collective identity is defined negatively as activism opposed to violence and extremism, while positively encouraging dialogue and integration, social responsibility, and preservation of faith. My research into the Dialogue Society and Mevlana Rumi Mosque shows that the movement's most committed supporters include owners of small businesses, professionals and working class people, as well as members of more prosperous backgrounds—a few very successful businessmen. Thus, the organizational development of the Hizmet Movement reinforces an earlier argument by McCarthy and Zald, according to which impoverishment, despair, and grievances are not sufficient to cause collective action organizations to grow.[193] Participants in the two Hizmet organizations are found to be purposively and rationally committed to the movement through value, material, and solidarity incentives. Some exit cases were also encountered, in which ex-participants shifted their interests toward other activities.

Material resources

As mentioned in Chapter Two, Gülen's definition of *sadaka* and *vakıf* makes *zakat* applicable to skills, knowledge, time, and wealth, as well

---

[192] That is, people participate in Hizmet according to the levels of their own interest and motivation.

[193] McCarthy and Zald, Resource Mobilization and Social Movements: A Partial Theory.

as efforts made in various community service activities, eliminating barriers of understanding and communication, prejudice, and stereotypes. By this means, the *vakıf* tradition has been extended beyond material and financial contributions to include contributions for dialogue and coexistence within societies.

Meanwhile, another important aspect of Hizmet mechanisms for accessing financial resources is its dependence on economic enterprises and transnational trade, in which its market for new books, products, and services extends beyond Turkish territory to almost every country where Hizmet is functioning. By creating its own market supply and a substantial part of its demand, the Hizmet Movement maintains its relation to Islamic notions of *sadaka* and *vakıf*, while actively engaging in the world market economy, where it transfers its social and moral capital into financial constituencies to fund different charity organizations.

In sum, strategic adaptivism, as explained above, provides a base for understanding possible mechanisms of resource mobilization as applied by the Hizmet Movement's organizations in two of their main spaces of action—community networking and community service. This study examined both macro and micro determinants of that process and according to these the Hizmet Movement in London has succeeded in relating its goals to those of its community, and hence has effectively mobilized moral, socio-organizational, human, and material resources.

The Islamic nature of Hizmet

While much national and international comment considers the Hizmet Movement, in general, to be a power for reconciliation between tradition, spirituality and modernity, some commentators approach the movement as a new version of extremist groups which are manipulated by "backward interior enemies," the Islamists, and "imperialist foreign forces."[194] Interestingly enough, the perception of a prominent threat posed by the movement is quite comparable to the debate about

---

[194] See Özdalga 2000 for a discussion of such commentary.

Dönme Jews in the early decades of the twentieth century.[195] The way some critics have questioned the identity of the movement, its participants' loyalty to nationhood, their financial power, and their foreignness/globalism has almost replicated the earlier debate about the *Dönme* Jews in the Turkish context, and reflects the historical and cultural peculiarity of such debates, namely, a conspiracy culture in the Turkish public sphere. Özdalga, a close observer of the movement, explains the "phantasmagoria" of the movement by ultra-secular critiques as "nourished by dread, bordering on panic, of religious reactionaries (*irtica*), combined with ignorance about what the Gülen community really does."[196]

For this reason, my study was organized around understanding the "know-how" of the Hizmet Movement. This perspective was intended to answer one main question: *How can the Hizmet Movement be classified in relation to the spectrum of Islamic movements?* While organizationally structured around the "betterment of human life," the Islamic nature of the Hizmet Movement is found in certain values that it upholds (which incidentally are also values common to other faiths and traditions) such as piety (*takva*), purity of intention and sincerity (*ihlas*), commitment (*adanmışlık*) and self-sacrifice (*fedakarlık*).[197] To that end, it represents a rational and professional type of collective action. For this reason I have used organizational and social movement theories for their ability to closely describe the movement's activism, in which the difference is found in the know-how rather than in the product it provides: education, commodities, media products or services.

The Anatolian background of the Hizmet Movement has deeply affected its transformation from a faith-centric *cemaat* confined to the

---

[195] The Dönme were a Jewish sect that lived under Ottoman rule in Salonika (now part of Greece) during the late 17th century. After the Ottoman Empire was forced to withdraw from lands in Greece and Eastern Europe, the Dönme (i.e., returning) Jews escaped religious oppression by migrating to Turkey's mainland—mainly to Istanbul, Edirne, and İzmir. Later, they converted, allegedly nominally, to Islam and were later accused of being one reason for the fall of the Ottoman Empire (Baer 2004).

[196] Özdalga, Secularizing Trends in Fethullah Gülen's Movement, 61.

[197] For further discussion of these points see Michel 2010.

Turkish platform of community service to its current form of a trans-national network of intellectuals, institutions, and businesses serving inclusively and seeking to involve people of different backgrounds. Moreover, its resolute drive toward inter-faith and inter-cultural dialogue has also attracted many non-Muslim activists to its activities. Therefore, it is clear that the Hizmet Movement is no longer a home-grown *cemaat*; rather, the "Islamic" and the "Turkish" features of the movement have begun to cede to the spiritual, the global, the modern and the humanistic. Put differently, this suggests that Hizmet has become, rather, a human-centric social community, or what Uluengin (2011) terms *"camia"* (collectivity), through which its religious and cultural character is incidentally reconstructed toward further diversity and globalism.

In this way, the Hizmet Movement disrupts traditional typologies of Islamic movements, especially the popular threefold typology: traditionalist/fundamentalist, modernist, and secularist. In fact, many researchers have criticized this typology and a number of attempts have addressed the necessity for a representative typology apart from the relational identification inherent in the classical proposition.[198] However, after the 9/11 attacks, the labeling of Islamic movements became even more controversial, with new terms gaining publicity and influence, such as neo-fundamentalism, neo-traditionalism, conservatism, Salafi reformism, reformist traditionalism, neo-modernism, post-modern fundamentalism, revivalism, reformism, modern piousness, and so on.[199] Furthermore, the fact that the Hizmet Movement, wittingly or otherwise, restructures the spectrum of Muslim activism further problematizes the question of "how to label" it.

To some of its close observers, the Hizmet Movement stands in contrast to political Islam and even Islamic movements in general. While Bulaç, Ergene, and Yilmaz maintain a description of the move-

---

[198] See, for instance, Rahman, Islamic Modernism; Haddad, The Islamic Alternative; Shepard, Islam and Ideology; Esposito, *The Oxford History of Islam*, 690; Voll, *Islam, Continuity and Change in the Modern World*; Ramadan 2003 in Auda, Maqasid Al-Shariah, 146.

[199] Ibid.

ment as "social Islam" and "civil Islam" respectively,[200] Yavuz considers the Hizmet Movement to be a society-centered, rather than a state-centric, Islamic movement.[201] Shared themes in these definitions are:

1) the Hizmet Movement is concerned with "everyday-life-based pious activism (…) viewing Islam as cultural capital; and use of associational networks to empower the community";[202]

2) rejection of direct involvement in politics;

3) endorsing a pacifist view of contentious politics and abiding by the rule of law;

4) endorsing a discourse friendly to democracy, modernity, and secularism; and

5) respecting national and state figures especially Atatürk, the Turkish national leader.

Building on these guidelines, I also found some of the premises of the study of Islamic movements inadequate to afford a full grasp of either the philosophy or applied mechanisms of the Hizmet Movement. At this point it is necessary to elaborate a number of assumptions briefly.

Firstly, the claim that there is a reactionary "resurgence," "revival," or "re-emergence" of Islamic movements as a result of European colonialism, frustration with modernization projects, education, and the print revolution. The socio-historical record of Hizmet, explained in Chapter Two, suggests rather an autonomous Islamic impulse in which the movement has succeeded in re-inventing its cultural and religious tradition[203] to fit within national and international contexts.

---

[200] Bulaç, The Most Recent Reviver in the 'Ulama Tradition; Ergene, The Future of Islamic Movement in the Arab World; Yilmaz, State, Law, Civil Society and Islam in Contemporary Turkey, 394.

[201] Yavuz, *Islamic Political Identity in Turkey*.

[202] Ibid., 28.

[203] Invention of tradition has been defined as "the process of formalization and ritualization, characterized by reference to the past, if only by imposing repetition" (Hobsbawm and Ranger, *The Invention of Tradition*, 4). It applies to Hizmet in the sense that some aspects of the Anatolian heritage, for instance, values of coexistence and tolerance, are formalized in forms of interfaith and intercultural dialogue institutions. By re-invention I refer to earlier and competitive tradition–modernity

In contrast to the "othering" and rejectionist stance of different Islamist movements toward the West, democracy, and secularity—either due to the West's "domination"[204] or based on profound ideological and historical grounds[205]—the Hizmet Movement does not align the West with religious affiliation or economic and political superiority. Its "other" is rather a more general materialist approach to human society and human-nature relationship, an approach whose proponents would view the Hizmet Movement's model of collective action as profoundly nonsensical.

Secondly, while Islamic movements are generally approached through what Euben terms the "structural-functionalist" approach,[206] the spread of the Hizmet Movement in both Turkey and around the world suggests an intrinsic appeal in its blend of intellectual and professional networking qualities rather than a specific contextual environment. This, however, does not suggest complete neglect of its socio-historical background, since it provides context for meaning systems to work. Finally, scholars in Islamic movements often share a focus on a set of ideologized standpoints—the rule of *shari'a*, the Islamic state,[207] reviving the "golden age," invention of traditions and the call to Islam;[208] however, modern education, dialogue, community services and media occupy the forefront of the focus in the Hizmet Movement.

The "motivational" role of the Islamic spiritual dimension of Hizmet has attracted a different set of labels, compared to those prevalent in Islamic movements; the movement has been described as a *neo-Sufist*,[209]

---

formulas that stand against the Hizmet Movement, yet with less intellectual, moral, financial and organizational resourcefulness.

[204] Hunter, *The Future of Islam and the West*, 114.

[205] Anderson in Esposito, *Political Islam*, 25.

[206] An approach that concerns itself with the functions and structures of Islamic activism rather than its constitutive values and concepts that provide intellectual 'functions' that lie beyond the traditional separation of religion and the public sphere life in Western societies. Euben, *Enemy in the Mirror*, 24.

[207] Burgat, *Face to Face with Political Islam*, 60.

[208] On these points see briefings by Eickelman and Piscatori, *Muslim Politics*, 30–3.

[209] Michel, The Gülen Movement.

modern *Sufist*,[210] "modernist,"[211] and "worldly ascetic's movement."[212] It is a case of community service deeply rooted in Islamic values and traditions while remaining, at least apparently, at arm's length from political engagement. It also manifests many conjunctions with modern philosophical stands on human dignity and rights. The individuation trend within the movement, reflected in its entrepreneurial basis and *hicret* concept, is balanced by notions of social responsibility and commitment.

Conclusion

My research into the Dialogue Society and Mevlana Rumi Mosque results in a number of "analytical generalizations."[213] Firstly, society-centered activism that focuses on broadening public consensus and support can successfully mobilize resources for different projects. Secondly, connecting local constituencies to media, academia, and local authorities through consistent and transparent channels multiplies local support and trust in the social movement organization. Thirdly, rejection of political partisanship, maintaining equal distance from all political parties, while acquiring government support for community service projects, develops effective communication channels and multiplies the resource base of the movement organizations.

Although case studies do not always provide a sound basis for generalized findings, further research into the London-based Hizmet Movement could apply comparative research techniques to different applications of the Hizmet philosophy across the world and could even extend to comparison with the activities of other Islamic movements, particularly the Muslim Brotherhood. The fieldwork experience of this study suggests that the Hizmet Movement is best researched through group and focus interviews to minimize both time and financial costs.

---

[210] Ibid.

[211] Fuller, *The Future of Political Islam*, 59.

[212] Özdalga 2003, 62.

[213] Yin, *Case Study Research*, 15.

A number of challenges were encountered while doing this study. Firstly, while the movement intentionally makes itself visible to social, academic, and political actors, the immense fluidity of its structure and its "invisibility" in the sense described in Chapter One,[214] raises concerns as to how its organizations and initiatives are developing, in which directions, and on which socio-economic bases. An identification of the research subject and demarcation of its insider-outsider elements is unattainable due to the numerous forms in which Gülen's philosophy is applied, and due to the multi-faceted loosely networked structure of Hizmet activities. This raises a claim by the researcher that Hizmet is becoming a "lifestyle" for rising numbers of social groups with different backgrounds, religions, and cultures. Secondly, the use of secondary resources in the Hizmet Movement case is unreliable. The mounting body of research on the movement authoritatively shapes any further research and is deeply bound to the researcher's position, background, and the availability of resources: time, money and language skills. In such a way, the Hizmet Movement presents a case where research "tribes" occur around different positions *vis-à-vis* its activism, with little empirical grounds and much speculation. This study reveals the need to move toward further understanding of the movement's actual work.

While it provides a provisional finding on the two most active organizations in London, the end of this study should not signal a conclusion to researching its subject. Rather, it sheds light on potential areas for further research, such as how the clientele profile differs in each organization; longitudinal analysis of sample service recipients over a number of years in order to assess the extent to which Hizmet goals are achieved and in which ways they influence the broader society; how accountability and transparency are achieved and maintained within the organizations; and how traveling to participate in different Hizmet projects affects the personal and career development of participants. Finally, since my research on the Hizmet Movement organizations concludes that there exists a positive correlation between soci-

---

[214] See especially Methodology section.

ety-centered activism and resource mobilization, the recent uprisings in the Arab world suggest the need to conduct further comparative studies with protest and Islamic political movements, to examine the conditions under which political activism can broaden or limit the mobilization constituencies of a Social Movement.

Glossary of Turkish and Arabic Terms

adanmışlık	commitment, dedication
al-ʿamal al-salih	good deeds
Alevi	Alevism is a religious practice drawing on Shi'a and Sufi sources. However, nowadays in Turkey, for a significant number of people who identify as Alevis it is a group or cultural identity, rather than a religious practice.
ʿalim (pl. *ʿulema*)	scholar of Islam
camia	collectivity
cemaat	In the Turkish tradition, a social group gathered around a prominent scholar of religious knowledge, with the aim of acquiring religious knowledge. It also extends to collective social and economic activities by its participants.
cem evi	place of worship for Alevi people
da'wa	inviting to Islam
diğergamlık	altruism
ezan	call to prayer
fedakarlık	self-sacrifice
fiqh	Islamic jurisprudence
hicret	journey, migration
Hijri calendar	Islamic calendar dating from the Prophet's migration
himmet	personal commitment and enthusiasm to carry out a project
hizmet	altruistic service for the betterment of human life

Hizmet Movement	loosely connected organizations and local circles that are inspired by the teachings of Fethullah Gülen in their social activism
hoca	teacher, particularly of religion (term implying good character)
hoşgörü	seeing the best in others
iftar	meal to break the sunrise to sunset fast in Ramadhan
ihlas	purity of intention and sincerity
i'layı kelimetullah	glorifying the word of God
iman	faith
istişare	collective consultation
Kadiri	a major *Sufi* order
kalam	theology
kermes	food or book fair, small-scale fund-raising event
konak	traditional mansion house typical of the Ottoman period
maarife-i kavmiye	national consciousness
madhhab	school of Islamic law (Turkish: *mezhep*)
madrasa	traditional educational institution in Muslim societies (Turkish: *medrese*)
mafsada	mischief
maqasid (sg. maqsid)	purposes, objectives, or principles that lie behind Islamic rulings
maslaha	fulfillment of the good; public well being or interest
muhasebe	self-criticism, self-accounting
mürid	spiritual seeker or student in a Sufi order
mürşid	spiritual guide or teacher in a Sufi order
mütevelli heyeti	board of trustees/directors
Nakshibendi	(or Naqshbandi) a major Sufi order

Nurculuk	term used to denote all those who read Said Nursi's work *Risale-i Nur* as a form of devotion
Risale-i-Nur	"The Message of Light", title of a lengthy thematic commentary on the Qur'an by the scholar Said Nursi
sadaka	voluntary alms-giving
shari'a	moral and legal code based on Islamic sources, the reintroduction of which is a goal of many political Islamist movements in Muslim countries
sohbet	local friendship circles that meet and read passages from Fethullah Gülen's writings on various topics, e.g., literary, theological or scientific issues
Sufism, Sufi	the inner spiritual aspect of Islam, focusing on practices for purifying the heart of all sin and of all reprehensible inner states
takva	fear of God, piety
tarikat	order, path, or way in Sufism, with initiation, and inner hierarchy and specific spiritual practices (in addition to all the other rites of Islam). Usually arranged in lodges (tekke). In Turkey, the most common are the *Nakshibendi* and *Kadiri* orders. These are not sects— there is mutual recognition between them and with all the schools of law (*madhhab*).
tebliğ/tablighi	teaching about religion
tefsir	Qur'anic exegesis (conducted according to a rigorous set of guidelines including thorough knowledge of previous exegeses and other Islamic sources)
temsil	religion in practice, embodiment of ideals, teaching by example

tevazu	the spiritual practice of humility
'ulema	see *'alim*
ummah	term used for the entire worldwide community of Muslims
usul-u hadith	science or knowledge of hadith (accounts of the Prophet's words and deeds), including meaning, chains of transmission, and reliability of individuals in the chains
vakıf	charity foundation, still extant Turkish tradition from the Ottoman period
verme tutkusu	passion for giving
zakat	annual charitable donation made by Muslims, due on 2.5% of wealth according to Islamic law

Bibliography

Albayrak, Ismail. *Mastering Knowledge in Modern Times: Fethullah Gülen as an Islamic Scholar*. Blue Dome Press, 2011.

Altinay, Levent and Eser Altinay. Determinants of Ethnic Minority Entrepreneurial Growth in the Catering Sector. *The Service Industrial Journal*, 26(2) [2006]: 203–221.

———. Marketing Strategies of Ethnic Minority Businesses in the United Kingdom. *The Service Industrial Journal*, 28(8) [2008]:1183–1197.

Atay, Rifat. Reviving the *Suffa* Tradition. In *Muslim World in Transition: Contributions of the Gülen Movement*, 459–472. London: Leeds Metropolitan University Press, 2007.

Ansari, Humayun. *The Infidel Within: Muslims in Britain Since 1800*. C. Hurst and Co. Publishers, 2004.

Auda, Jasser. *Maqasid Al-Shariah: A Beginner's Guide*. IIIT, 2008.

Ayoob, Mohammed. *The Many Faces of Political Islam: Religion and Politics in the Muslim World*. University of Michigan Press, 2008.

Baer, Marc D. The Double Bind of Race and Religion: The Conversion of the Dönme to Turkish Secular Nationalism. *Comparative Studies in Society and History*, 46(4) [October 2004]: 682–708.

Ball, Stephen J. Initial Encounters in the Classroom and the Process of Establishment. In *Pupil Strategies*, edited by P. Woods. London: Croom Helm, 1980. Cited in Hammersley, Martyn and Paul Atkinson. *Ethnography: Principles in Practice*. 2nd ed. Routledge, 1994.

Baykusoglu, Serkan. The Effects of Language and Culture on the Achievement of Turkish-Speaking Students in British Schools: 1990s to 2004. *Journal of Muslim Minority Affairs*, 29(3) [2009]:401.

Bhatti, Faqir Muhammad. *Turkish Cypriots in London*. Birmingham: Centre for the Study of Islam and Christian–Muslim Relations, 1981.

Bishkek and Istanbul Global Muslim Networks: How Far They Have Travelled. The Economist, 2008. Available at: www.economist.com/node/10808408?story_id=10808408.

Bourdieu, Pierre. *Distinction: A Social Critique of the Judgement of Taste*. Harvard University Press, 1987.

Bourdieu, Pierre and Loïc J.D. Wacquant. *An invitation to reflexive sociology*. University of Chicago Press, 1992.

Brewer, John D. *Ethnography*. Open University Press, 2000.

Bryman, Alan. *Social Research Methods*. 3rd ed. Oxford: Oxford University Press, 2008.

Buechler, Steven M. *Women's Movements in the United States: Woman Suffrage, Equal Rights, and Beyond*. Rutgers University Press, 1990.

Bulaç, Ali. The Most Recent Revival in the 'Ulama Tradition. In *Muslim Citizens of the Globalized World: Contributions of the Gülen Movement*, edited by R. A. Hunt and Y. A. Aslandoğan, 101–121. The Light, 2007.

———. *Din, Kent ve Cemaat ve Fethullah Gülen Örneği*. Ufuk Publishing, 2008.

Bulmer, Martin. *Sociological Research Methods: An Introduction*. 2nd ed. Palgrave Macmillan, 1984.

Burgat, François. *Face to Face with Political Islam*. I.B.Tauris, 2002.

Burgess, Robert G. *The Research Process in Educational Settings: Ten Case Studies*, Taylor and Francis, 1984. Cited in Brewer, John D. *Ethnography*. Open University Press, 2000.

Campbell, John L. Where Do We Stand? Common Mechanisms in Organizations and Social Movements Research. In *Social Movements and Organization Theory*, edited by Gerald F. Davis, Doug McAdam, W. Richard Scott, Mayer N. Zald, 41–69. Cambridge: Cambridge University Press, 2005.

Cantori, Louis J., Marcia Hermansen, and David B. Capes. *Muslim World in Transition: Contributions of the Gülen Movement*. Leeds Metropolitan Press, 2007.

Carroll, Jill B. *A Dialogue of Civilizations: Gülen's Islamic Ideals and Humanistic Discourse*. Tughra Books, 2007.

Çelik, Gürkan. *The Gülen Movement: Building Social Cohesion Through Dialogue and Education*. Eburon Publishers, 2011.

Çetin, Muhammed. *The Gülen Movement: Civic Service Without Borders*. Blue Dome Press, 2010.

Change Institute. The Turkish and Turkish Cypriot Muslim Community in England: Understanding Muslim Ethnic Communities, United Kingdom, London, Communities and Local Governments, 2009.

Cilingir, Sevgi. Identity and Integration among Turkish Sunni Muslims in Britain. *Insight Turkey*, 12 (1) [2010]:103–122.

Curtis, Russell L. and Louise A. Zurcher, J. Stable Resources of Protest Movements: The Multi-organizational Field. *Social Forces*, 52 (1973):53–60.

Denzin, K. *Sociological Methods: a Sourcebook*. Transaction Publishers, 2006.

Diani, Mario. Networks and Participation. In *The Blackwell Companion to Social Movements*, edited by D. A. Snow, S. A. Soule, and H. Kriesi, 339–359. Wiley-Blackwell 2004.

Ebaugh, Helen R. *The Gülen Movement: A Sociological Analysis of a Civic Movement Rooted in Moderate Islam*. Springer, 2009.

Edwards, Bob and John D. McCarthy. Resources and Social Movement Mobilization. In *The Blackwell Companion to Social Movements*, edited by D. A. Snow, S. A. Soule, and H. Kriesi, 116–152. Wiley-Blackwell, 2004.

Eickelman, Dale F. and James Piscatori. *Muslim Politics*. New ed. Princeton University Press, 2004.

Enneli, Pınar, Tariq Modood, and Harriet Bradley. *Young Turks and Kurds: A Set of "Invisible" Disadvantaged Groups*. Joseph Rowntree Foundation, 2005.

Aykan Erdemir and Ellie Vasta. *Differentiating Irregularity and Solidarity: Turkish Immigrants at Work in London*. United Kingdom, Oxford: ESRC Centre on Migration, Policy and Society, 2007.

Erdoğan, Latif. *Fethullah Gülen Hocaefendi 'Küçük Dünyam.'* 1997 accessible in Turkish at: www.hikmet.net/content/category/19/3791/12/.

Ergene, Enes. *Geleneğin Modern Çağa Tanıklığı: Gülen Hareketinin Analizi*. Istanbul: Yeni Akademi Publishing, 2005.

———. *Tradition Witnessing the Modern Age: An Analysis of the Gülen Movement*. Somerset, New Jersey: Tughra Books, 2008.

———. The Future of Islamic Movements in the Arab World: Comparative Experiences with the Gülen Movement. In *Islamic Movements in Turkey and the Experience of the Gülen Movement*. Arab League, Cairo. The Centre for Civilizational Studies and Dialogue between Cultures, Cairo University, 2009.

Esposito, John L. *Political Islam: Revolution, Radicalism, or Reform*. Lynne Rienner Publishers, 1997.

———. *The Oxford History of Islam*. Oxford University Press, USA, 2000.

Euben, Roxanne L. *Enemy in the Mirror: Islamic Fundamentalism and the Limits of Modern Rationalism: A Work of Comparative Political Theory*. Princeton University Press, 1999.

Freeden, Michael. *Ideologies and Political Theory: A Conceptual Approach*. Oxford University Press, 1996.

Freilich, Morris. *Marginal Natives: Anthropologists at Work*. Harper and Row, 1970. In M. Hammersley, and P. Atkinson. *Ethnography: Principles in Practice*. 2nd ed. Routledge, 1994.

Fuller, Graham E. *The Future of Political Islam*. Palgrave Macmillan, 2004.

———. *The New Turkish Republic: Turkey as a Pivotal State in the Muslim World*. United States Institute of Peace Press, 2007.

———. *A World Without Islam*. Little, Brown and Company, 2010.

Gamson, William A. *The Strategy of Social Protest*. Wadsworth Publishing, 1990.

Gamson, William A., Bruce Fireman, and Steven Rytina. *Encounters With Unjust Authority*. Dorsey Press, 1982.

Geertz, Clifford. *The Interpretation of Cultures*. Basic Books, 1973.

George, V. and G. Millerson. The Cypriot Community in London. *Race and Class*, 8(3) [1967]: 277–292.

Gerlach, Luther P. and Virginia H. Hine. *People, Power, Change: Movements of Social Transformation*. Bobbs-Merrill, 1970.

Gilsenan, Michael. *Recognizing Islam*. New ed. Croom Helm Ltd, 1983.

Göle, Nilüfer. *Forbidden Modernities*. I.B. Taurus, 2008.

Gong, Li. Ethnic Identity and Identification with the Majority Group: Relations with National Identity and Self-esteem. *International Journal of Intercultural Relations*, 31 [2007]:503–523.

Gülen, M. Fethullah. *Buhranlar Anaforunda İnsan*. Istanbul: Nil Yayınları, 1980.

———. Ruh'un Zaferi. *Sızıntı*, 54(5) [1983]:383.

———. Introduction. In Said Nursi. *Epitomes of Light: Mathnawi Al-Nuriya*. Izmir: Kaynak Yayınları, 1999.

———. *Örneklerin Kendinden Bir Hareket*. Nil Yayınları, 2000. Available at: tr.fGülen.com/content/category/30/9/3/.

———. *Ruhumuzun Heykelini Dikerken*. Nil Yayınları, 2004a.

———. *Toward a Global Civilization of Love and Tolerance*. NJ: The Light, 2004b.

———. *The Statue of Our Souls: Revival in Islamic Thought and Activism*. NJ: Tughra Books, 2005a.

———. *Gurbet Ufukları*. Gazeteciler ve Yazarlar Vakfı (JWF) Yayınları, 2005b.

———. *Key Concepts in the Practice of Sufism: Emerald Hills of the Heart*. NJ: Tughra Books, 2006a.

———. *The Spirit of Jihad and its Truth in Islam (Rouh Al-Jihad wa Haqiqatuhu fi Al-Islam)*. Cairo: Nil Publishing, 2006b.

———. *Ümit Burcu*. Istanbul: Gazeteciler ve Yazarlar Vakfı Yayınları, 2006c.

———. *Gönüllüler Hareketi ile Dünya Yeşerecek*. 2010. Available at: tr.fGülen.com/content/view/18383/11/ [Accessed June 6, 2011].

Haddad, Yvonne. The Islamic Alternative. *The Link*, 15(4) [1982]:1–14.

Hammersley, Martyn and Paul Atkinson. *Ethnography: Principles in Practice*. 2nd ed. Routledge, 1994.

Harrington, James C. *Wrestling with Free Speech, Religious Freedom, and Democracy in Turkey: The Political Trials and Times of Fethullah Gülen*. University Press of America, 2011.

Heirich, Max. *Change of Heart: A Test of Some Widely Held Theories about Religious Conversion*. Centre for Research on Social Organization, University of Michigan, 1973.

Hobsbawm, Eric and Terence Ranger. *The Invention of Tradition*. Cambridge University Press, 1983.

Struder, Inge R. *Do Concepts of Ethnic Economies Explain Existing Minority Enterprises? The Turkish Speaking Economies in London.* London: Department of Geography and Environment, London School of Economics, 2003.

Tayfun, Atay. "Ethnicity Within Ethnicity" Among Turkish Speaking Immigrants in London. *Insight Turkey,* 2010. Available at: www.faqs.org/periodicals/201001/1988411641.html.

Tedik, Fatih. Gülen Movement as an Integration Mechanism for Europe's Turkish and Muslim Community: Potentials and Constraints. In *Muslim World in Transition: Contributions of the Gülen Movement,* 230–245. London: Leeds Metropolitan University Press, 2007.

———. Motivating Minority Integration in Western Context: The Gülen Movement in the United Kingdom. In *Peaceful Coexistence: Fethullah Gülen Initiatives in the Contemporary World.* London: Leeds Metropolitan University Press.

The Dialogue Society. *Interview with Simon Robinson.* London, 2010. Available at: www.dialoguesociety.org/advisors.html [Accessed March 4, 2011].

Thomson, Mark. *Immigration to the United Kingdom: The Case of Turks.* United Kingdom: Sussex Centre for Migration Research, University of Sussex, 2006.

Thomson, Mark, Nicola Mai, and Janroj Y. Keles. *"Turks" in London: Shades of Invisibility and the Shifting Relevance of Policy in the Migration Process.* United Kingdom: Sussex Centre for Migration Research, University of Sussex, 2008.

Tomlin, Lara. Meet Fethullah Gülen, the World's Top Public Intellectual. *Foreign Policy,* 2008. Available at: www.foreignpolicy.com/articles/2008/08/03/meet_fethullah_guelen_the_worlds_top_public_intellectual.

Toğuslu, Erkan. Gülen's Theory of Arab and Ethical Values of Gülen Movement. In *Muslim World in Transition: Contributions of the Gülen Movement.* London: Leeds Metropolitan University Press, 2007.

Turam, Berna. *Between Islam and the State: The Politics of Engagement.* Stanford University Press, 2006.

Uğar, Etga. Religion as a Source of Social Capital? The Gülen Movement in the Public Sphere. In *Muslim World in Transition: Contributions of the Gülen Movement,* 152–163. London: Leeds Metropolitan University Press, 2007.

Uluengin, Hadi. Gülen Movement: A Religious Community (*cemaat*) or A Social Community (*camia*). *Hurriyet.* 06/04/2011. Available at:en.fGülen.com/press-room/columns/3715-hadi-uluengin-hurriyet-Gülen-movement-a-religious-community-or-a-social-community.

Ünal, Ali. *Advocate of Dialogue: Fethullah Gülen.* Fountain Publishing, 2000.

Vahide, Şükran. Bediüzzaman Said Nursi and the Risale-i Nur. In *Globalization, Ethics and Islam: The Case of Bediüzzaman Said Nursi,* edited by I. Markham and I. Ozdemir, 3–37. England: Ashgate Publishing Limited, 2005.

Voll, John O. *Islam, Continuity and Change in the Modern World.* Syracuse University Press, 1994.

Weber, Max. *Economy and Society: An Outline of Interpretive Sociology*. University of California Press, 1978.

Weller, Paul. Religions and Social Capital. Theses on Religion(s), State(s), and Society(ies): With Particular Reference to the United Kingdom and the European Union. *Journal of International Migration and Integration*, 6(2) [2005]:271–289.

Wiktorowicz, Quentin. Islamic Activism and Social Movements Theory: A New Direction for Research. In *Shaping the Current Islamic Reformation*, edited by B. A. Roberson, 187–212. Routledge, 2003.

Winlow, Steve, and Simon Hall. *Violent Night: Urban Leisure and Contemporary Culture*. Berg, 2006. Cited in Van Der Neut, P., Change and Continuity on the South Coast: Young People Identity, Consumerism and Employment. MPhil dissertation. United Kingdom: University of Cambridge, Sociology Department, 2009.

Woellert, Kroehnert et al. Ungenutzte Potentiale: Zur Lage der Integration in Deutschland. Berlin: Berlin-Institut fuer Bevoelkerung und Entwicklung, 2009. Cited in Karcher, A. Integrating Turks in Germany: The Separation of Turks from German Society, Discrimination against Turks in the German Labor Market and Policy Recommendations to Integrate Turks into German Society. Honors Thesis. Public Policy Studies, 2010. Accessed on June 11, 2011, on: dukespace.lib.duke.edu/dspace/bitstream/handle/10161/2315/Karcher%20 Albert%20Honors%20Thesis.pdf?sequence=1.

Yavuz, M. Hakan. Cleansing Islam from the Public Sphere. *Journal of International Affairs*, Columbia University, School of International Public Affairs, 2000.

———. *Islamic Political Identity in Turkey*. Oxford University Press, USA, 2003.

———. The Case of Turkey (On Secularism and Religion). In *Daedalus*. American Academy of Arts and Sciences, 2003.

———. *The Emergence of a New Turkey: Democracy and the AK Party*. University of Utah Press, 2006.

Yavuz, M. Hakan and John L. Esposito eds. *Turkish Islam and the Secular State: The Gülen Movement*. Syracuse University Press, 2003.

Yavuz, M. Hakan. and Roberta Micallef. Turkish Diaspora and Islam in Turkey. *Journal of Muslim Minority Affairs*, 24(2) [2004]: 209–374.

Yavuz, M. Hakan and Nihat A. Ozcan. Crisis in Turkey: the Conflict of Political Languages. *Middle East Policy*, 14(3) [2007]:118–135.

Yilmaz, Ihsan. Marriage Solemnization Among Turks in Britain: the Emergence of a Hybrid Anglo-Muslim Turkish law. *Journal of Muslim Minority Affairs*, 24(1) [2004]: 57.

———. State, Law, Civil Society and Islam in Contemporary Turkey. *The Muslim World*, 95(3) [2005]:385–412.

———. Beyond Post-Islamism: A Critical Analysis of Turkish Islamism's Transformation toward Fethullah Gülen's Stateless Cosmopolitan Islam. In *Islam in the Age of Global Challenges: Alternative Perspectives of the Gülen Movement*. Georgetown University, Washington, DC, 2008. Available at: www. rumiforum.org/academic-papers/beyond-post-islamism-a-critical-analysis-of-the-turkish-islamisms-transformation-toward-fethullah-guelens-stateless-cosmopolitan-islam.html.

Yin, Robert K. *Case Study Research: Design and Methods*. Sage Publications, 2009.

Zald, Mayer N. and Roberta Ash. Social Movement Organizations: Growth, Decay and Change. *Social Forces*, 44(3) [1966]:327–341.

Zald, Mayer N. and John D. McCarthy. *Social Movements in an Organizational Society: Collected Essays*. Transaction Publishers, 1990.